D1450362

Relationship Conflict

NEUMANN COLLEGE

COLLEGE
LIBRARY

ASTON, PA. 19014

SAGE SERIES ON CLOSE RELATIONSHIPS

Series Editors
Clyde Hendrick, Ph.D., and
Susan S. Hendrick, Ph.D.

In this series...

Relationship Conflict

Conflict in Parent-Child, Friendship, and Romantic Relationships

Daniel J. Canary
William R. Cupach
Susan J. Messman

Sage
Series
on Close
Relationships

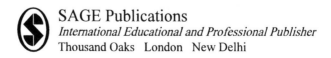

SAGE Publications
International Educational and Professional Publisher
Thousand Oaks   London   New Delhi

BF
637
.I48
C36
1995

Copyright © 1995 by Sage Publications, Inc.

All rights reserved. No part of this book may be reproduced or utilized in any form or by any means, electronic or mechanical, including photocopying, recording, or by any information storage and retrieval system, without permission in writing from the publisher.

For information address:

SAGE Publications, Inc.
2455 Teller Road
Thousand Oaks, California 91320
E-mail: order@sagepub.com

SAGE Publications Ltd.
6 Bonhill Street
London EC2A 4PU
United Kingdom

SAGE Publications India Pvt. Ltd.
M-32 Market
Greater Kailash I
New Delhi 110 048 India

Printed in the United States of America

Library of Congress Cataloging-in-Publication Data

Canary, Daniel J.
    Relationship conflict: Conflict in parent-child, friendship, and romantic relationships / Daniel J. Canary, William R. Cupach, Susan J. Messman.
        p. cm.—(Sage series on close relationships)
    Includes bibliographical references and index.
    ISBN 0-8039-5129-9 (cloth: alk. paper).—ISBN 0-8039-5130-2 (pbk.: alk. paper)
        1. Interpersonal conflict. 2. Conflict (Psychology) 3. Intimacy (Psychology) 4. Interpersonal relations. I. Cupach, William R. II. Messman, Susan J. III. Title. IV. Series.
    BF637.I48C36 1995
    302.3′4—dc20   95-4968

This book is printed on acid-free paper.

95 96 97 98 99 10 9 8 7 6 5 4 3 2 1

Sage Production Editor: Tricia K. Bennett

Contents

Series Editors' Introduction

When we first began our work on love attitudes more than a decade ago, we did not know what to call our research area. In some ways, it represented an extension of earlier work in interpersonal attraction. Most of our scholarly models were psychologists (though sociologists had long been deeply involved in the areas of courtship and marriage), yet we sometimes felt as if our work had no professional "home." That has all changed. Our research has not only a home but also an extended family, and that family is composed of relationship researchers. During the past decade, the discipline of close relationships (also called personal relationships and intimate relationships) has emerged, developed, and flourished.

Two aspects of close relationships research should be noted. The first is its rapid growth, resulting in numerous books, journals, handbooks, book series, and professional organizations. As fast as the field grows, the demand for even more research and knowledge seems to be ever increasing. Questions about close, personal relationships still far exceed answers. The second noteworthy aspect of the discipline of close relationships is its interdisciplinary nature. The field owes its vitality to scholars from communication, family studies and human development, psychology (clinical, counseling, developmental, social), and sociology, as well as other disciplines such as nursing and social work. It is this interdisciplinary wellspring that gives close relationships research its diversity and richness, qualities that we hope to achieve in the current series.

The **Sage Series on Close Relationships** is designed to acquaint diverse readers with the most up-to-date information about various topics in close relationships theory and research. Each volume in the series covers a particular topic or theme in one area of close relationships. Each book reviews the particular topic area, describes contemporary research in the area (including the authors' own work, when appropriate), and offers some suggestions for interesting research questions and/or real-world applications related to the topic. The volumes are designed to be appropriate for students and professionals in communication, family studies, psychology, sociology, and social work, among others. A basic assumption of the series is that the broad panorama of close relationships can best be portrayed by authors from multiple disciplines, so that the series cannot be "captured" by any single disciplinary bias.

Conflict is a natural and even inevitable aspect of most ongoing, close relationships. So the issue that differentiates successful from unsuccessful relationships is not whether there is conflict but, rather, how it is handled. The current volume, *Relationship Conflict*, skillfully portrays developmental or "healthy" conflict as well as destructive or "unhealthy" conflict in our most significant personal relationships: parent-child, friendship, and romantic relationships. By taking an interdisciplinary focus with a strong developmental thread, the authors—Daniel Canary, William Cupach, and Susan Messman—expertly lead the reader through a substantial amount of current research and theory to help increase understanding of conflict's legitimate place in the human experience.

CLYDE HENDRICK
SUSAN S. HENDRICK
SERIES EDITORS

Preface

How individuals manage interpersonal conflict dramatically affects their own development and their personal relationships. Although many students recognize the importance of conflict, few understand what it is and how it functions to preserve or to erode close relationships. More precisely, and in spite of the prevalence of interpersonal conflict, many of us cannot indicate the important interaction behaviors that accompany relational harmony or turbulence. We want to provide a synthesis for advanced students that would reflect the diverse literature on conflict in close relationships.

The purpose of this book, then, is to examine the question, "What does conflict look like in various close relationships?" To address this question, we examine how social scientists conceptualize and measure conflict in parent-child, friendship, and romantic relationships. Although such an undertaking appears straightforward, the accomplishment of it requires loyalty to diverse research in social and developmental psychology, communication, sociology, and other related disciplines.

Our purpose emerged from a desire to reflect different and interdisciplinary literature on conflict. Virtually hundreds of social scientific research books and articles on the topic reveal an amazing lack of integration regarding knowledge about interpersonal conflict in various types of close relationships, despite the effort of many researchers to work from a broad knowledge base. Although we readily acknowledge the limits of our own understanding on the topic, a representative synthesis of research approaches to the study of conflict in close relationships still appears warranted.

Few researchers explore conflict processes across various personal relationships. Instead, most of us focus on a particular kind of relationship in our research, or we pursue research objectives that entail scope conditions suggesting a certain kind of interpersonal involvement. Efforts to research different relationships have generated a wealth of information on the topic of conflict in close relationships, which is a positive outcome. One regretful outcome of this focus on particular relationships concerns a lack of coherence on the simple question guiding this book. The answer to the question of what conflict looks like in various kinds of close relationships also changes across disciplines.

Or does it? Are there "points of connection" between conflict and close relationships in general? We believe that there are, at least enough so as to permit inferences. However, we recognize that people correctly immersed in their own portion of the picture may feel frustrated that we did not elaborate in a particular way on that portion. We hope the reader understands that our goal is to represent a diverse body of research concerning different relationship forms. We realize that our goal means that we omit some detail. Nevertheless, we think this decision presents the reader with a fuller grasp of interpersonal conflict processes across relationship types as presented in several fields.

A crucial point of convergence occurs in the examination of interaction behaviors. That is, in order to talk about how people in close relationships have and manage conflict, researchers eventually discuss how conflict is interpersonally accomplished through interaction behavior or interpersonal communication. As Hinde (1976) noted, "To describe a relationship, it is necessary to describe the interactions that occur—that is, their context and their quality" (p. 4). Accordingly, we focus on processes central to conflict interaction between two people in close relationships.

By *close relationships,* we refer to relationships characterized by knowledge of the partner, interdependence, and inability to replace the relational partner (vs. replacing a store clerk, or any other social relationship) (Duck, Lock, McCall, Fitzpatrick, & Coyne, 1984; Perlman & Fehr, 1987). We discuss three generic types that we see represented in the conflict literature: parent-child, friendship, and romantic (dating and married) relationships.

We do not attempt to review all the relevant theory and research. Such a review would be exhausting, to use Roloff's (1987) turn of phrase. Comprehensive and insightful reviews on the conflict activities can be found elsewhere with regard to particular kinds of relationships, including parent-child (e.g., Dunn & Slomkowski, 1992), friendship (e.g., Hartup, 1992), and romantic (e.g., Schaap, Buunk, & Kerkstra, 1988). Instead our goal is to provide a representative survey and commentary on empirical research to reveal some links among these literatures.

‰ Preview of Chapters

Chapter 1 presents our assumptions and attempts to locate definitions of interpersonal conflict. Toward this end, it explores dimensions of definitions and theoretical orientations on interpersonal conflict. This initial chapter reveals much variation in definitions and theoretical orientations to interpersonal conflict.

Chapter 2 reviews popular survey and observational measures of conflict. The reader will again discover immense differences in operational definitions of conflict, reflecting the conclusion in Chapter 1 that researchers, by and large, do not explicitly agree on the nature of the phenomenon. Our position is that *both* survey and observational approaches are needed, depending on the scholar's research purpose. However, we do provide a set of advantages and disadvantages for each approach.

Chapter 3 concerns conflict in parent-child relationships. The research regarding parent-child relationships casts conflict in a child development framework. Researchers take interest in conflict for what it says about the maturation of the child, especially in recent conceptions of bilateral influences of mother and child. This literature also reflects two different conflict activities: one involving the young child trying to master his or her social world and one featuring the adolescent trying to understand changes due to puberty while asserting him- or herself as an individual. We also discuss the direct and indirect effects of parental conflict, including psychological adjustment outcomes related to parental conflict and divorce.

Chapter 4 discusses conflict between friends. This literature begins with a discussion of conflict between young acquaintances, friends, and siblings, again stressing the bridges between conflict behaviors and individual development. This chapter is organized on literature specific to particular cohorts, stressing how conflict patterns between friends change over important friendship periods. More specifically, our discussion focuses on conflict between early childhood friends, middle childhood friends, adolescent friends, and adult friends.

Conflict in romantic involvements is presented in Chapter 5. Hundreds of studies have examined romantic conflict, many with an eye on connecting various conflict behaviors to relational quality or stability. This research provides insights into the productive and destructive relational features of interpersonal conflict. Perhaps here (more than in Chapters 3 and 4), we attempt to represent the literature, in lieu of providing a comprehensive account. The sheer number of articles published on the topic of conflict in romantic relationships is daunting.

Chapter 6 concludes this book with four points of connection between conflict and close relationships. Accordingly, Chapter 6 provides a forum for a few generalizations about conflict in close relationships. Of course, we do not miss the opportunity to suggest some interdisciplinary avenues for future research.

❧ Acknowledgments

Several people deserve mention for their help and support to us during the completion of this project. First, several people provided technical assistance. Sue DeWine (Director, School of Interpersonal Communication, Ohio University) provided us with resources to photocopy articles. Tara Emmers, Parrish McIntosh, Rebecca Smith (all from Ohio University), and Larry Erbert (University of Iowa) provided several citations as part of research projects with the lead author. Molly deLaval-Hixson (Ohio University) helped type our initial reference list. Each of these people made our task of assembling the necessary materials easier.

We also wish to acknowledge the editors of the series, Susan and Clyde Hendrick, for their generous and friendly support and patience as we proceeded through different phases of this book (and as we have moved around the country). We most appreciate their careful and immediate feedback on the initial draft. Their attention to meaning and detail is marvelous. Several fine editors at Sage promoted and dramatically improved our manuscript. We owe a debt of gratitude to C. Terry Hendrix for his encouraging us along the way, to Dale Grenfell for her diligent editing, and to Tricia Bennett for her expert management of the production of the book. As authors, we have benefited from the series editors' sage advice, as well as those who work in Thousand Oaks, California.

DANIEL J. CANARY
WILLIAM R. CUPACH
SUSAN J. MESSMAN

1

The Nature of Conflict in Close Relationships

For several reasons, conflict in interpersonal contexts enjoys a high research priority among scholars examining close relationships. First, the management of conflict tests the character of relationships perhaps more rigorously than do other types of interaction. Partners in quality relationships manage conflicts through positive interaction behaviors, which include collaborating with each other and disallowing escalation of anger into aggression, rejecting withdrawal as a viable management strategy, and avoiding or changing destructive behavioral patterns and cycles (e.g., Gottman, 1994; Sillars & Wilmot, 1994).

Second, interpersonal conflict is central to individuals' development (Valsiner & Cairns, 1992). As Shantz (1987) observed, "Conflict is a central concept in virtually every major theory of human development" (p. 283). Dunn and Slomkowski (1992) showed that conflict and development of social understanding connect in four important areas: in understanding others' feelings and intentions, in using or grasping social conventions and rules that guide behavior, in children's use of strategic communication, and in knowledge of different categories relevant to interpersonal relationships. In other words, conflict plays a critical role in the ways in which people come to understand how social interaction functions to promote individual needs within personal relationships.

Third, relational parties must learn to negotiate conflict because the risks of psychologically or physically hurting each other because of disputes are real and emotional. According to one review (Marshall, 1994), approximately 20% of people experienced a violent episode (e.g., hitting, etc.) in their romantic relationships within the previous year. Productive management of conflict helps prevent physical and psychological aggression in close relationships (e.g., Infante, Chandler, & Rudd, 1989; Margolin, Burman, & John, 1989; for a review, see Lloyd & Emery, 1994). Parents who manage conflict constructively are less likely to neglect or abuse their children and thereby become less apt, directly or indirectly, to "teach" them such behaviors (Minuchin, 1992). Continued research on this topic outlines some of the important boundaries between constructive and destructive conflict behaviors.

Finally, as a pervasive social activity, interpersonal conflict merits continued examination. Many scholars recognize that interpersonal relationships inherently require conflict, despite the negative images it conjures up for participants (e.g., Hocker & Wilmot, 1991). For example, Gottman (1994) observed that "nearly all the research on marital interaction has involved the observation of conflict resolution" (p. 66). Psychological, communicative, and sociological properties linked to conflict processes reveal much about people and how they relate to each other. Accordingly, to understand people as social and relational participants, we need to understand conflict—its causes, its communication, and its consequences.

In this chapter, we first offer four assumptions that we hold about conflict in close relationships. These assumptions indicate why we emphasize what we do in this book. Following the assumptions, we discuss definitions of conflict in close relationships according to episodic and behavioral variations. These definitions indicate much divergence in conceptualizations of conflict and conflict management behaviors. Finally, to indicate how scholars locate the construct of conflict in different areas, we review popular theoretical views on conflict in close relationships.

⋗ Research Assumptions

Four assumptions accompany our analysis: The first three assumptions indicate our view of the link between conflict and close relationships, and the final assumption points to parameters on our review.

First, we believe that the potential for conflict resides in the very activity of two people relating to each other. Conflict on the surface level in close, personal relationships reflects subsurface difficulties in how two highly interdependent people "negotiate" their rights, responsibilities, and assessments of each other. As interdependence increases, potential areas for conflict increase (Braiker & Kelley, 1979).

Second, how people manage conflict reveals much about the nature of their relationships. More specifically, conflict interaction behaviors strongly determine evaluations of the messages, attributions about the communicator, the partner's subsequent behavior, and, ultimately, the relationship (e.g., Burggraf & Sillars, 1987; Canary & Cupach, 1988; Harvey, Wells, & Alvarez, 1978; Sillars, 1980b). Assessments of the relationship and patterns of interaction that maintain the relational system, in turn, affect how partners manage conflict between them (e.g., Gottman, 1979; Robin & Foster, 1989; Weiss & Dehle, 1994). In a word, conflict interaction both affects and is affected by features of close relationships.

Third, understanding conflict in close relationships requires attention to issues germane to different types of close relationships. For example, an issue critical to parent-child and friendship conflict concerns how children develop their communication skills. However, the issue of individual development almost disappears in studies of adult conflict. Instead, in adult conflict, attributions for causes of conflict gain more attention. We do not imply, however, that such segmentation of issues according to relational types necessarily represents a positive move. Yet we cannot escape the fact that relationships vary in their functions and characteristics, and these differences probably affect how conflict emerges and progresses.

Finally, we are most informed by social scientific examinations of conflict within personal relationships. We opt for empirical theory and research to provide information about interpersonal conflict. Hence, we do not discuss philosophical, political, or critical views on the nature of conflict, as important as they are. Nor do we review any studies that focus on individual phenomena (e.g., intrapsychic conflict), unless interpersonal processes are directly implicated. Nor do we examine intergroup or "social" conflict, unless (again) a direct connection is made to interpersonal processes. Finally, we will deemphasize studies that do not focus on conflict per se but concern related areas, such as aggression (e.g., Hartup, 1974), compliance-gaining (e.g., Fitzpatrick & Winke, 1979), and competition (e.g., Hughs, 1988). The following section provides ways of setting parameters used to define interpersonal conflict behavior.

♨ Defining Interpersonal Conflict

Definitions of conflict collectively present a surreal image that evokes mystery rather than certainty about the subject. Although many agree that conflict involves some incompatibility between people (Deutsch, 1973), additional differentiations lack consensus (Weider-Hatfield, 1993). In one dissertation, Prinz (1976, cited in Hall, 1987) found eight different definitions of interpersonal conflict derived from the empirical literature: [conflict as] interruptions, disagreements, tension, defensive versus supportive communication, anxiety tension and emotions, antagonism, negative interpersonal expressiveness, and contradictions between verbal and nonverbal messages. As Weiss and Dehle (1994) observed, "A precise, all-purpose definition of *conflict* is still lacking" (p. 95).

A lack of consensus about the term *conflict* works against understanding the role of conflict. As Shantz (1987) observed, too much breadth in definitions of conflict has led to problematic conceptual ambiguity. Similarly, Hartup and Laursen (1993) noted that variation in definitions makes comparisons across studies complicated and potentially misleading. In addition, we must separate conflict from related domains of behavior.

Interpersonal conflict occurs at several levels of experience (Braiker & Kelley, 1979). For example, Cahn (1990) proposed that conflict occurs at three levels: "specific disagreements" (e.g., argument over a particular issue), "problem-solving discussion" (e.g., bargaining), and "unhappy/distressed relationships" (i.e., patterns of interaction that indicate distressed couples). A quandary immediately arises with regard to this differentiation. The quandary is this: Conflict at one level does not necessitate conflict at another level, but conflict at one level may become manifest at another level. For example, relational level problems may or may not emerge as disagreements about particular behaviors and issues. Moreover, partners' conflict exchanges about particular behaviors and issues can easily affect relational harmony.

The diversity of definitions and levels of interpersonal conflict defy simplification. Oversimplification would only muddle a murky view. A more comprehensive position appears to be one that differentiates the topic while including different conceptualizations and levels.

≈ Dimensions for Characterizing Definitions

In our view, definitions of conflict vary in terms of their episodic and behavioral frames of reference. First, definitions differ in the extent to which they reference a distinct type of interaction or episode. In other words, definitions vary in the claim that people engage in an interaction type called a "conflict episode." In this view, conflict has a recognizable beginning and end, typified by disagreement and/or negative affect. Second, definitions vary in the extent to which particular kinds of behavior qualify as conflict management behavior. Some researchers explicitly reference specific conflict behavior, whereas other researchers remain ambiguous about the kinds of behavior that constitute conflict management (or conflict resolution) behaviors. Of course, researchers have not relied on these episodic or behavioral frames, and their definitions may overlap or evolve over time. Still, these dimensions serve a pedagogical function by helping us identify different kinds of conflict definitions.

Based on this 2×2 distinction, four definitional categories emerge, each implying what conflict is. Figure 1.1 portrays these four definitional types, which are briefly reviewed in turn at this point.

1: Nonepisodic/Nonspecific. Category 1 definitions of conflict are not confined to a particular kind of interaction episode, nor do they limit conflict to specific kinds of behavior. Instead, conflict is viewed as a fluid phenomenon, permeating different interaction types in many behavioral forms. As Sprey (1971) claimed, "The family process *per se* is conceived of as a continuous confrontation between participants with conflicting—though not necessarily opposing—interests in their shared fate" (p. 722).

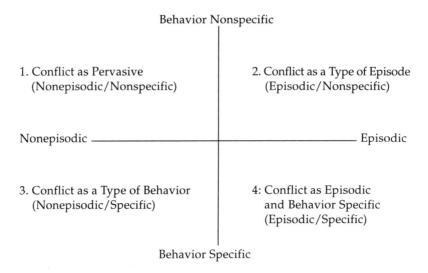

Figure 1.1. Categories of Interpersonal Conflict Definitions

Conflict as episode-free and behaviorally nonspecific allows re-searchers to focus on behaviors not bound by episodic considerations, such as how adolescents and parents variously show relational stress (Montemayor, 1986). As Cahn (1992) observed, "In the context of intimacy, moreover, conflict is more than a disagreement, incompatibility between partners, or partner opposition; it is an enduring or persistent element of interaction. Since it endures, it can also change and develop in form over time" (p. 3). Hence, Category 1 definitions include a wide range of situations and behaviors.

In addition, Category 1 definitions can reference any behavior that is made in the company of the partner as conflict. For example, researchers focusing on behaviors that discriminate happy from un-happy couples often include behaviors that do not appear to involve disagreement, though they may be effective predictors of couple status (e.g., Gottman, 1979; Margolin, 1990). In other words, couples' discussions—especially those involving problem solving or problematic issues—can reflect relational (dis)satisfaction. Accordingly, behaviors that couples enact in such discussions qualify as conflict, according to some researchers.

An obvious criticism of this approach concerns its primary advantage: It is too inclusive. Clearly, conflict often arises from the overall context of daily interactions that involve ongoing relational ups and downs. How such interactions unfold varies tremendously. However, Category 1 definitions obscure precisely when interactions are characterized by, or even involve, particular conflict management behaviors. For example, the importance of "tracking" (i.e., attending to) the partner is not limited to disagreements. Attending to one's partner can also reflect an overall style of interaction, regardless of any actual or perceived conflict.

Some researchers (e.g., Sillars, 1986) preempt being overly inclusive by asking participants to indicate the extent to which a problem also entails disagreement. For example, a couple may experience tension because the husband does not show the wife enough affection. If both husband and wife agree that he does not show enough affection, then they do not appear to have any conflict, although they certainly do have a problem. Of course, if the husband claims he provides enough affection and the wife claims he does not, then clearly conflict exists on this issue. Unfortunately, without such reports of (dis)agreement, researchers may not know when a discussion reflects disagreement over particular incompatibilities or reflects more global relational problems. It is certainly feasible to consider the behavioral management of conflict apart from the more general and chronic communication enveloped in ongoing relational troubles. Category 2 definitions reduce some of this ambiguity by qualifying conflict as a particular episode.

2: Episodic/Nonspecific. Conflict is sometimes defined as an interaction episode, typically marked by significant disagreement indicated by negative emotions or other indexes of intensity. For example, Strawbridge and Wallhagen (1991) examined conflict among adult peers as "a clash or strong feeling of resentment" (p. 772). Similarly, Jenkins and Smith (1991) required that a conflict last at least 5 minutes and involve raised voices. These definitions indicate that interpersonal conflict is inherently an unpleasant event. Adopting a more neutral conception, Shantz (1987) defined conflict as "time-distributed social episodes having their own microgenetic features" (pp. 285-286). These definitions imply that interpersonal conflict largely occurs within the minds of two individuals who may be upset with each other for a brief period or over longer periods of time.

Several assumptions embedded within episodic definitions of conflict are evident. First, social actors must be able to identify particular exchanges as conflictual. In other words, such episodes are isolated from other routines that the relational parties enact so that conflicts are seen by conflict parties as discrete events. Research suggests that, when cued with synonyms such as "quarrel" (Shantz & Hobart, 1989), people do readily recall conflict episodes (Laursen, 1993). Second, explicit behaviors need not be present for an interpersonal conflict to occur. Although this may appear counterintuitive, consider that people may feel angry or otherwise upset by the partner and so perceive an instance of "conflict," although for several reasons (e.g., memory loss; Sillars, Weisburg, Burggraf, & Zietlow, 1990), they may be unable to articulate precisely how the conflict episode began or continued. Finally, Category 2 definitions include many behaviors that indicate instances of negative affect.

Conflict episodes that unfold gradually, so that their boundaries remain unclear to either or both parties, are , by definition, enigmatic. Conflict-as-episodic definitions may suggest cues, such as negative emotions, to identify conflict interactions more precisely. But these definitions do not necessarily specify *how* people manage conflict behaviorally to evidence their internal battles. Lack of behavioral specificity is critical to the extent that the occurrence of conflict episodes may not be as important as how actors actually behave during conflict. As Straus (1979) noted, "A key factor differentiating what the public and many professionals regard as 'high conflict families' is not the existence of conflict *per se*, but rather, inadequate or unsatisfactory modes of managing and resolving the conflicts which are inherent in the family" (p. 85). Explicating specific conflict behaviors characterizes Category 3 definitions of conflict.

3: Nonepisodic/Specific. Category 3 definitions do not distinguish conflict as an interaction episode, but they do concern specific kinds of conflict management behavior. In other words, conflict occurs whenever particular kinds of behavior occur. For example, Foster (1987) provided a behavioral definition of "clinical conflict" as "recurring negative exchanges that repeat without resolution" (p. 254). Likewise, and using a systems approach, Bavelas, Rogers, and Millar (1985) defined conflict as three consecutive dominant messages.

A popular Category 3 definition in the family literature centers on opposition, which provides an episode-free but a behavior-specific definition (e.g., Eisenberg, 1992; Vuchinich, 1987, 1990). As Vuchinich (1990) claimed, conflict is a "distinctive speech activity. . . . In verbal conflict, participants oppose the utterances, actions, or selves of one another in successive turns at talk" (p. 118). In other words, conflict potential occurs when one person opposes the partner in some way. If the partner then counters the opposition, then the potential conflict becomes an actual conflict. But if the partner does not offer a counter, then the opposition remains unchallenged and no conflict occurs. But people may often counter oppositions. Vuchinich (1987) found that 64% of initial oppositions are countered, indicating behavioral conflict, and that a remarkable 91% of oppositional moves occur in successive turns.

Certain behavioral features of opposition further specify how conflict emerges. For example, Eisenberg and Garvey (1981) noted that the "opposer" represents the person who initially and behaviorally resists the opposee (the person challenged), yet the burden of proof rests on the opposee. That is, the opposee must counter with justifications or other persuasive strategies whereas the opposer only has to restate his or her initial opposition. In addition, conflict stops once opposition ceases, for example, after about three opposition-free conversational turns (Vuchinich, Emery, & Cassidy, 1988) or after 30 seconds of unopposed interaction (Hay & Ross, 1982). In short, Category 3 definitions of conflict reside in the specific interaction behaviors and exchanges of the participants.

Perhaps the major drawback to Category 3 definitions concerns a *lack of consensus* about the specific behaviors that define conflict interaction. As mentioned previously, there are many behavioral definitions of conflict, including opposition, dominance moves, interruptions, confirming/disconfirming behaviors, and the like. Accordingly, studies relying on Category 3 definitions are not directly comparable in their findings: One researcher's study of conflict may be dismissed as tangential by a different conflict researcher. In this regard, oppositional exchanges may not represent any significant disagreement or incompatibility as much as a *mode* of responding, for example, in controlling or domineering ways.

4: *Episodic/Specific.* In this final category, conflict management refers to specific communication behaviors enacted in particular episodes involving disagreement. For example, Hall (1987) appears to have combined the specific behavior of disagreement with the episodic characteristic of negative affect: [Conflict, in contrast to opposition, entails] "greater hostility, aggression, and emotion than does disagreement. . . . Conflict between a parent and a teenager means disagreement coupled with hostilities" (p. 768). We would again indicate, however, that people do not automatically communicate in a negative manner during conflict. Indeed, research reveals that people use alternative strategies to manage their incompatibilities.

Examining conflict strategies stresses general approaches people take to manage conflict episodes. Whereas *strategies* refer to the general approaches used to achieve an interaction goal, *tactics* concern the particular behaviors that institute the strategy (Newton & Burgoon, 1990a). Three general strategies correspond roughly to the notion that people work with each other, against each other, or away from each other (e.g., Davitz, 1969; Horney, 1945): *integrative* (working with the partner); *distributive* (working against the partner); and *avoidant* (working away from the partner) (e.g., Canary & Cupach, 1988; Canary & Spitzberg, 1989; Sillars, 1980a, 1980b). Researchers have identified other strategic approaches, most of which maintain a distinction between cooperative and competitive conflict (e.g., positive vs. negative codes; constructive vs. destructive strategies; prosocial vs. antisocial behaviors; confirming vs. disconfirming messages).

Research involving *styles* (i.e., individual tendencies to manage conflict episodes a particular way) also illustrates Category 4 concepts of conflict. Although styles research has dominated the organizational domain, it has made few inroads into the literature on close relationships. One reason for this is that research examining styles views conflict as a modal tendency to act similarly in different situations. This focus can distract attention from situational and partner constraints on behavior, which represent important topics in personal relationship research.

As with Category 1, the strength of Category 4 definitions doubles as its primary weakness: The specificity in Category 4 definitions overly delimits the scope of interpersonal conflict. It appears simplistic to assume that people reserve certain behaviors to manage conflict episodes only when they arise. Still, one could view behavior functionally, suggesting that in particular conflict episodes a cooperative strategy (for example) effectively pools resources primarily to manage the incompatibility, whereas in nonconflictual encounters cooperation functions primarily to maintain the relational status quo. In addition, relational tensions transcend particular episodic encounters. Sorting the ways that conflict at the relational level is manifested in the daily, routine interactions of couples presents an important definitional issue as well as a pragmatic research concern.

In sum, although conflict definitions vary in terms of episodic and behavioral specificity, most researchers appear to agree that interpersonal conflict involves some incompatibility, even if such incompatibility reflects relational discord. Many researchers specify communicative behaviors, whereas others define the subject as an episode involving hostility. Most researchers, however, do not require that conflict entail overt hostility, because people manage conflict using a variety of strategies and tactics, only some of which actually demonstrate hostility. Nevertheless, the idea that conflict entails more than casual disagreement deserves noting.

To represent further researchers' understanding of conflict, we move the discussion from definitions to theories. One's theoretical view assists in locating the construct, and it emphasizes particular features of the phenomenon (Fisher, 1978). A brief survey of alternative theoretical approaches indicates different ways of thinking about, and important research issues concerning, interpersonal conflict.

❧ A Sample of Theories About Conflict in Close Relationships

The presumed connection between theory and research in the area of conflict has been doubted. For example, Montemayor (1983) reviewed research on parent-adolescent conflict and concluded that there was "virtually no connection between the theories and the research in this area" (p. 87). Similarly, in their comprehensive anthology on child conflict, the editors Shantz and Hartup (1992) decried a "lack of fit" between what theorists mean by conflict and how researchers actually study conflict management behaviors.

Despite these observations, theoretical developments have emerged and reveal very different conceptualizations of conflict. These conceptualizations suggest where researchers find answers to their questions, suggesting where the phenomenon resides (i.e., scope parameters). These are reviewed at length elsewhere. For example, Hall's (1987) review indicated three theoretical approaches: psychoanalytic, systems, and social learning. Cahn's (1992) review of marital conflict distinguished systems-interactionist, cognitive-exchange, and rules-based approaches. Weiss and Dehle's (1994) review stressed cognitive and behavioral models; specifically, the physiological affect model by Gottman and Levenson, behavioral exchange models, and attribution models. Our objective at this point is not to review theories but rather to show how various theory types affect one's understanding of the proper domain of interpersonal conflict. Accordingly, we briefly present three different approaches: developmental, cognitive (social exchange and attribution), and interactional. These were selected because they provide clear alternative conceptualizations of conflict.

Developmental Theories

A lion's share of the research on parent-child conflict uses a developmental perspective. As Dunn and Munn (1985) explained, changes in cognitive and affective development become "particularly clear in children's behavior during family conflict. The intense encounters among children, their siblings, and their parents over conflicts of interest and transgression of rules, provide a context" (p. 480) in which researchers can assess child development.

Textbooks (e.g., Vander Zanden, 1980), scholarly books (e.g., Cantor & Khilstrom, 1987), and review articles (e.g., Shantz, 1987) have attested to the divergent views regarding individual development. Notwithstanding such diversity and complexity, particular theories on parent-child conflict provide coherence to the research (Hall, 1987), many of which feature developmental factors. Selman's theory clearly illustrates such a developmental approach.

Selman (1980) discussed peer conflict as it reflects development of child social perspective taking (see also Flavell, 1968, regarding role taking). Selman stressed social perspective taking as the sine qua non of individual development. Selman offered five levels of social perspective taking roughly linked to age groupings:

Level 0: Undifferentiated and Egocentric Perspective Taking (about age 3 to 6). Children do not differentiate physical from psychological reality, and they impose their view of the social world onto others.

Level 1: Differentiated and Subjective Perspective Taking (about age 5 to 9). Here, children separate physical from psychological properties of people. But the child's perspective of relations is still only one-way (i.e., self affects other *or* others affect self).

Level 2: Self-Reflective/Second-Person and Reciprocal Perspective Taking (about age 7 to 12). At this level, children look at self from others' point of view and realize that others do the same. Two-way reciprocity characterizes the child's understanding of social relations (i.e., self affects other *and* others affect self).

Level 3: Third-Person and Mutual Perspective Taking (about age 10 to 15). At this level, children see others as complex mixtures of attitudes and behaviors. Moreover, the child can see self and other as an interdependent system. Influence is mutual so that self and other simultaneously affect each other, and this can also be consciously realized by both parties.

Level 4: In-Depth and Societal-Symbolic Perspective Taking (about age 12 to adult). At the highest level of perspective taking, thoughts and actions are psychological though not necessarily caused or even understood. Hence, people can be viewed as internally inconsistent. Social relations are understood at multiple levels of meaning, for example, as interpretations of actions as legal, moral, ethical, or conventional. At this point, one abstracts a view of behavior from the position of a "generalized other." (Mead, 1934)

As Selman (1980) has shown, at Level 0 children manage conflicts through evasion or force. Use of these management strategies reflects how children at this level do not separate the physical behaviors from psychological intentions. Accordingly, the child might engage in leaving the situation, hitting the other person, or other remedies that are fixed on the immediate problem without concern for psychological or relational consequences.

At Level 1, children view conflict as one-way influence, which indicates that they search for the one cause and seek to remedy it. For example, conflicts can be viewed as the result of yelling; in order to resolve the conflict, one simply stops yelling and apologizes.

At Level 2, when influence is seen as bidirectional, children attempt to accommodate each other's desires to achieve their own goals. Selman noted that because intentions are often attributed as causes for behavior at this stage, children may focus on whether or not someone really *means* a particular response. Hence, children begin to focus more on attributions for intent (e.g., degree of sincerity underlying one's conciliation).

At Level 3, conflicts are seen as mutually constructed events that should be managed to both parties' satisfaction. Conflict can also concern superficial or deep issues, with closer relationships providing greater latitude in management behaviors. Selman (1980) summarized conflict management behaviors at this level: "The emphasis of Level 3, then, appears to be on *active* interpersonal communication and sharing, and on verbal or mental rather than physical-action resolutions" (p. 112).

Finally, Level 4 conflicts entail a more realistic view of relationships. For example, relationships do not require overbonding. In addition, at Level 4, children exercise the notion that intrapsychic conflicts comprise the root cause of interpersonal conflicts. Moreover, nonverbal and verbal messages provide means to manage conflicts, as one of Selman's (1980) 16-year-old participants explained:

> Well, you could talk it out, but it usually fades itself out. It usually takes care of itself. You don't have to explain everything. You do certain things and each of you knows what it means. But if not, then talk it out. (p. 113)

Although Selman focused on peer conflict, his theory is also applicable to other relationships to the extent that we can tie children's conflict behavior to their capabilities of social perspective taking (Flavell, 1968). In fact, Clark and Delia (1976) and Delia, Kline, and Burleson (1979) found that children's hypothetical persuasion strategies involving their mothers reflected advances in social perspective taking abilities. The extension to older populations constitutes an easy hurdle, to the degree that adults' social perspective taking promotes productive management of conflict (Burleson & Samter, 1994).

Cognitive Approaches

Conflict researchers have also emphasized how adults make sense of conflict. Two general theories representing this class are social exchange and attribution.

Social Exchange Theory. Social exchange theories adopt a financial metaphor to explain people's disagreement about scarce resources (for a review, see Roloff, 1981). In social exchange terminology, conflict occurs because in close relationships, interdependent parties share outcomes and depend on each other's actions to achieve valued resources. In terms of interdependence theory (Kelley, 1979; Kelley & Thibaut, 1978), people have conflict regarding their "mutual fate control" and "mutual behavioral control." In other words, people may disagree about the outcomes they receive due to the *exchange* of resources as well as difficulties in the *coordination* of their activities (Braiker & Kelley, 1979).

A lack of conflict should occur in relationships that are both rewarding and equitable (Hatfield, Traupmann, Sprecher, Utne, & Hay, 1985; Van Yperen & Buunk, 1990). Conflict occurs most frequently in relationships lacking in personal rewards or in those characterized by inequity. In either case, the individual attempts to arrive at a profitable and fair reward system, and, if attempts to do so fail, then they may "leave the field" (Adams, 1965). For example, Edwards and Brauburger (1973) argued that adolescents increase their reward systems outside the family, thereby becoming less reliant on resources of exchange within the family. Edwards and Brauburger found that adolescents with high reward alternatives experienced higher amounts of family conflict, higher amounts of parental negative statements (e.g., nagging, scolding, and yelling), but less physical punishment.

Conflict researchers also rely on exchange theory in viewing micro-level behaviors as rewards or costs (e.g., Parke, 1979; Vuchinich, 1984). Accordingly, praise, compliments, and the like represent rewards, whereas oppositions, teasing, and the like constitute costs, which suggests that the ratios of relational rewards and costs should include communicative processes, including how partners manage their conflicts. For example, one could identify relational inputs (or rewards/costs experienced during interaction) versus individual inputs or what each person brings to the relational system, such as financial status, opportunities gained or lost, and so on (Hatfield et al., 1985).

Attribution Theory. Attribution theory references social actors' explanations for events. Fincham, Bradbury, and Scott (1990) observe, "The bulk of the research on cognitions in marriage has focused on attributions or explanations that spouses make for marital events" (p. 125).

Relationship researchers most often focus on people's attributions for relational problems, which have been reviewed at length elsewhere (e.g., Bradbury & Fincham, 1990; Fincham et al., 1990; Harvey, 1987; Weiss & Dehle, 1994).

Much of the attribution research concerns dimensions of attributions, in particular the dimensions of *internality, globality,* and *stability,* among others. Not surprisingly, the literature reveals that dissatisfied people are more likely to attribute the causes of marital problems to factors that reflect internal, global, and stable factors. The most uniform support has been found for globality (Bradbury & Fincham, 1990); dissatisfied (vs. satisfied) couples generalize the causes of particular problems. Moreover, attributional dimensions appear to overlap (Bradbury & Fincham, 1990). For example, to the dissatisfied wife, the reason her husband does not show affection derives from his selfishness (an internal and stable explanation), which also indicates the global inferences of why he does not perform his share of household duties, why he avoids communication, and why he neglects the children.

Some research links attributions to conflict interaction. Sillars (1980a, 1980b) found that roommates were more likely to engage in distributive behaviors and to reciprocate distributive messages when they attributed the cause of conflict to the other. Consistent with the actor-observer bias (i.e., people overestimate the internal and controllable causes of others' behavior), Canary and Spitzberg (1990) found that assessments of partner competence were powerfully affected by perceptions of partners' conflict behavior, but self-assessments of competence were less affected by one's own conflict behavior. Consistent with the salience bias (i.e., active and negative behaviors are more salient than inactive and positive behaviors), research indicates that people are most sensitive to distributive conflict behaviors, then avoidance, then cooperative integrative messages (Canary & Spitzberg, 1990; Sillars, Pike, Jones, & Murphy, 1984).

Relying on attribution theory, Harvey and colleagues (e.g., Harvey, Orbuch, & Weber, 1990; Harvey, Weber, Galvin, Hustzi, & Garnick, 1986; Weber, Harvey, & Orbuch, 1992) have examined accounts that people offer for relational problems. According to Harvey, Orbuch, and Weber (1990), accounts reveal attributions about traumatic relational events in seven phases: Conflict and dissolution represent *traumatic events,* which lead to an *outcry* of emotions. These, in turn, lead to *denial* in such forms as avoidance. If denial proves ineffica-cious, then people feel flooded, or a state of *intrusion*. People then confide their accounts to others in the *working through* stage. Next, *completion* involves acceptance of one's story for the event. Finally, *identity change* occurs when one's story is fully accepted and works to change the account-giver over time. The clear implication for a defi-nition of conflict concerns the fact that interpersonal conflict escapes the confines of the dyad—interpersonal conflicts (especially large ones) also provide interesting, explanatory stories to outside friends and family (Weber et al., 1992).

Interactional Approaches

Interactional researchers have focused on conflict by analyzing observed behavioral sequences, often comparing satisfied/adjusted couples to dissatisfied/maladjusted couples (e.g., Gottman, 1979; Margolin & Wampold, 1981; Schaap, 1982; Ting-Toomey, 1983a). These theories operate from the premise that couple systems are defined by microlevel interaction behavior, typically witnessed in particular sequences. The issue, then, is to identify sequences that correspond to relational well-being (i.e., relational stability or satisfac-tion) (Weiss & Dehle, 1994).

For example, in a summary paper, Gottman (1982) described four patterns that characterize dysfunctional couples: *cross-complaining, counterproposal, negative metacommunication,* and *negative mind reading.* Cross-complaining references a pattern wherein one person offers a complaint in response to the partner's initial complaint; for example, "I wish you would clean up this house now and then" is followed by "Yeah, well, I wish you would cook more often." Some sort of validation—where one offers acknowledgment of the com-plaint—is more functional (Gottman, 1982). Counterproposals re-fer to exchanges of proposals, as in "Let's get a pizza and watch a video." "No, let's get out for the night." Gottman argued that contract-ing presents a functional alternative response here ("OK, we can watch a movie tonight, but let's go dancing this weekend"). Although metacommunication can clarify points of view, too much of the nega-tive kind distracts partners from the issue, as Gottman's (1982) exam-ple shows:

> **H:** You're interrupting me.
>
> **W:** I wouldn't have to if I could get a word in edgewise.
>
> **H:** Oh, now I talk too much. Maybe you'd like me never to say anything.
>
> **W:** Be nice for a change.
>
> **H:** Then you'd never have to listen to me, which you never do anyway.
>
> **W:** If you'd say something instead of jabbering all the time, maybe I would listen. (p. 112)

Finally, mind reading functions positively or negatively, depending on the nonverbal affect accompanying it (Gottman, 1982). For example, the statement "You always underestimate how long projects will take you" can reflect an attitude of concern or contempt. Such nonverbal affect helps determine how verbal messages are to be interpreted by participants and coded by researchers (see also Chapter 2).

In order to help organize interactional process issues, Sillars and Wilmot (1994) presented five dimensions that can be used to characterize structural properties of conflict interaction sequences: *variety*, or types of different messages enacted; *continuity*, or the number of issues raised; *symmetry*, or the extent to which the partners reciprocate each other's behaviors; *stationarity*, or the behavioral phases couples engage in, either within or between conflict episodes; and *spontaneity*, or the extent to which partners monitor and censor their messages. Sillars and Wilmot's analysis implied that the most functional conflicts involve a mixed proportion of these sequences; in other words, functional conflict interaction involves a wide variety of message behaviors that emphasize the issues at hand, a thorough (but not obsessive) discussion of salient issues, a reciprocal matching of the partner's cooperative (but not competitive) interaction behaviors, flexible phases of interaction, and a balance of self-monitoring and spontaneous tactical use.

ஆ Conclusions

People experience conflict in their most important, close relationships. How people manage their conflicts affects their relationship quality, personal development, and risk of interpersonal violence. In researching how conflict progresses in close relationships, we assume that conflict is part and parcel of close involvements, reveals the character of those relationships, concerns different facets in alternative relationships, and is best understood by attending to social scientific theory and research.

In reading the literature, we were struck by a lack of convergence on the term *conflict*. To lend coherence to the topic, we propose that definitions vary to the extent that they reference particular episodes and particular behaviors. In short, some researchers define conflict very generally, without reference to particular instances or manifestations of conflict, whereas others are more precise as to what conflict entails. Although we prefer specificity because it eases our task of identifying conflict process elements, we also acknowledge that conflicts extend beyond single episodes and emerge in a variety of actions. In addition, alternative theoretical orientations imply different foci for the study of conflict.

Research on children's conflicts (i.e., parent-child and peer) has used a variety of theories. The early developmental models of Freud, Erikson, and Piaget have been replaced in the contemporary research literature by social learning theory and systems theory. Developmental approaches provide a foundation for understanding children and adolescent conflict.

Although the development of children and adolescents has received careful attention in the conflict literature, the development of adults has garnered relatively very little. The message one gets is that the truly important life stage differences stop at early adulthood, so that after adolescence, conflict issues and behavioral responses remain free of developmental concerns. However, the scarce research on life stages and conflict has revealed that younger couples express themselves more than passive older couples, who differ significantly from middle-aged couples in their conflict interactions (Levenson, Carstensen, & Gottman, 1994; Sillars & Wilmot, 1989; Zietlow & Sillars, 1988). Theoretical research that examines adult change is needed for a complete account of how individual development relates to conflict management factors and behaviors.

Cognitive approaches have underscored mental constructions of conflict, implying that the proper domain of interpersonal conflict resides in the mind. Research on attributional points of view has supported this emphasis (Canary & Spitzberg, 1990; Doherty, 1981). For example, Harvey et al. (1978) found strong support for the contention that partners are egocentric in their attributions of problems;

that is, they appear to project their take on the issues onto others, despite several discrepancies between partners' attributions. In addition, the issue of equity (or similar concerns for relational equality) reflects an important general concern of fairness and can be assessed in terms of costs and rewards, inputs and outcomes, and so on.

Still, interpersonal conflict requires attention to the dyadic system (Roloff, 1987). In this light, research linking cognitive features to interpersonal interaction (especially in observational analyses) should stress how attributions, expectations, and the like are tied to interaction behavior. Importantly, conflict researchers can compare the relative influences of microlevel exchanges of behavior with more macrolevel issues of fairness (e.g., financial inputs, opportunities gained or lost, etc.) to predict their relative effects on relational quality and stability.

Interactional approaches to conflict have provided the greatest gains in predicting the stability of close relationships (Gottman, 1994). The expression and reciprocation of specific forms of negative affect appear to have the most deleterious effects on relational well-being (see also Chapter 5). Of course, the interactional perspective presents the other side of the cognitive coin; in stressing the microscopic patterns of conflict to reveal the emergence of dyadic systems, cognitive dimensions are deemphasized. Fortunately, researchers have studied both cognitive and interactional aspects, sometimes concurrently.

We should mention that researchers sometimes combine theoretical approaches. An excellent example of this is Robin and Foster's (1989) "behavioral-family systems" model. In this theory, social learning theory and systems theory are used to explain adolescent conflict (see Chapter 3). Eclectic approaches provide elasticity to the boundaries of interpersonal conflict. Eclectic approaches often assume that conflict processes are so complex as to require multiple perspectives, especially in the desire to explain individual as well as system activities. We do not necessarily believe this, because eclectic models tend to sacrifice coherence of understanding for breadth. In other words, the primary difficulty in eclectic approaches concerns their ability to offer a coherent, well-synthesized account of more than one focus.

In sum, this first chapter has revealed different definitions of conflict in close relationships. Definitions differ in the extent to which they reference particular episodes and behaviors, and a 2×2 pedagogical model was offered to highlight these differences. Location of the conflict construct can also be derived by examining alternative theoretical views. Developmental, cognitive, and interactional approaches clearly point to alternative places where conflict can be found. Accordingly, the current literature defies a consistent frame of reference for understanding the nature of interpersonal conflict. At the same time, such divergence provides a wealth of knowledge about the topic, which we seek to represent in the following chapters.

Chapter 2 discusses methods for "observing" conflict in close relationships. Providing valid assessments of interpersonal conflict is not an easy task, and researchers have expended considerable energy in this research enterprise. Not surprisingly, various survey and observational methods reflect the diversity of current conflict definitions and theoretical approaches.

2

Methods for Studying Conflict in Close Relationships

A s indicated in Chapter 1, conceptualizations of conflict vary. It is no surprise, then, that operational definitions of interpersonal conflict also differ substantially from one another. A larger epistemological issue affecting conflict research concerns what counts as a valid measure of behavior. For some researchers, only direct observation of interaction permits inferences about conflict behavior, although such interactions (of necessity) suffer from artificiality. For others, self-reports of conflict present a more valid option, despite the limitation that self-reports suffer from people's inability to recall precise accounts of their conflicts. The superiority of one approach over another does not reside in the approach itself (see Jacobson, 1985); instead, the superiority of the approach resides in its applicability to the research issue under investigation. Our contention in this chapter is that *both* approaches yield important information about conflict behaviors.

Self-report (or questionnaire) and observational approaches provide the bulk of scientific information about interpersonal conflict. These approaches are not mutually exclusive. For example, to measure various individual and system factors, Robin and Foster (1989) relied on both observational and questionnaire approaches. Most often, researchers combining approaches use questionnaires to categorize relationships into functional and dysfunctional types (Margolin, 1990) or to measure relevant outcomes of interaction, such as relational satisfaction (e.g., Margolin & Wampold, 1981). In this chapter, we sample the popular self-report and observational approaches for studying interpersonal conflict.

❧ Self-Report Procedures

Researchers most often have relied on self-report measures to study conflict in close relationships. In self-reports, social actors verbally indicate their experienced beliefs, feelings, attitudes, and perceptions of behavior. Researchers typically obtain such data with self-administered questionnaires, though personal interviews and diaries are also employed. We briefly present some approaches to collecting self-report conflict data. Next, we describe the content assessed by self-report measures and the relative advantages and disadvantages of such information.

Approaches to Collecting
Self-Report Conflict Data

Self-reports provide information pertinent to various levels of experience, ranging from the general and abstract to the specific and concrete. Questionnaires can help assess an individual's global conflict style or predisposition across contexts and relational targets (e.g., Brown, Yelsma, & Keller, 1981; Kilmann & Thomas, 1977). More narrowly, conflict perceptions can refer to a particular context (e.g., the workplace) or relationship (e.g., best friend). Some studies have required that individuals report on their reactions to multiple scenarios or relationships in an effort to determine individuals' consistency in their conflict behaviors across different situations (e.g., Conrad, 1991; Sternberg & Soriano, 1984; Utley, Richardson, & Pilkington, 1989). More specifically, individuals can report on their perceptions of particular episodes of conflict interaction. For example, Canary and

Cupach (1988) asked relational partners to recall a "recent" conflict they had with each other (i.e., within the previous 2 weeks). Likewise, Lloyd (1987, 1990a) had participants keep a structured diary record of all disagreements with their partner over a 2-week period.

Self-reports usually concern the research participant, that is, what the respondent did, how the respondent feels, what the respondent believes. Reports can also include how the respondent perceives a partner. When data are collected from dyads (i.e., both members of a relationship, such as father and daughter), the researcher can discern the relative congruence between partners' perceptions of a conflict and observe their role in (un)successful conflict management (e.g., Harvey et al., 1978; Knudson, Sommers, & Golding, 1980; Sillars et al., 1990).

The process of conflict in relationships over time is studied both prospectively and retrospectively. Prospective longitudinal designs involve soliciting data from participants on more than one occasion in order to obtain a temporal picture of conflict phenomena (e.g., Lloyd, 1990a; McGonagle, Kessler, & Gotlib, 1993). Retrospective designs typically involve respondents recalling feelings or behaviors in chronological fashion for particular stages or critical turning points in the history of the relationship (e.g., Braiker & Kelley, 1979; Lloyd & Cate, 1985). Prospective designs are preferred because they minimize some of the perceptual and recall biases that accrue to retrospective designs, and they permit more confident conclusions about the causal associations among variables. Because retrospective data derive from reconstructions collected at a single point in time, they may represent salient cultural scripts or stereotypes for behavior rather than accurate reports of actual events. However, the manner in which time distorts perceptions of a prior conflict or period of conflict holds research interest of its own, for example, in terms of how self-serving biases may distort one's recall to the person's advantage.

Content of Self-Report Measures

Self-report measures can assess a wide range of phenomena associated with conflict. We organize these measures loosely into two general categories: (a) perceptions of conflict behavior and (b) attitudes and beliefs regarding conflict.

Perceptions of Conflict Behavior. Self-report instruments do not assess actual conflict interaction. Instead, they represent an impression of perceived behaviors. A straightforward measure of frequency would assess the extent to which conflict occurs in a period of time. For example, Braiker and Kelley (1979) studied conflict in the development of close relationships using a retrospective interview technique, and a number of subsequent investigations have replicated and extended their findings. These studies typically employ a summed five-item scale labeled *conflict-negativity* (in some studies it is simply called *conflict*) to assess the perceived frequency of conflict in the relationship. Specifically, the items assess: the frequency and seriousness of arguments in the relationship, attempts to change bothersome things about the partner, the frequency of experiencing negative feelings (e.g., anger, resentment), and the extent to which negative feelings are expressed.

One of the most common approaches assesses an individual's typical, hypothetical style or general tendencies for handling conflict (e.g., Sternberg & Soriano, 1984). Several instruments are grounded in the seminal work of Blake and Mouton (1964, 1970), who focused on managerial behavior. Their scheme suggests that two fundamental dimensions underlie methods for handling conflict: attempting to satisfy one's own concerns and attempting to satisfy others' concerns. Crossing these two dimensions yields five styles of managing interpersonal conflict (see Figure 2.1): four polar styles and one style that reflects the midpoint of both dimensions.

Several measures of these styles have been developed specifically for the organizational (i.e., work) context, although usually they can be adapted for other contexts. One of the most popular style measures has been the Management of Differences Exercise (MODE) instrument developed by Kilmann and Thomas (1977; see also Kabanoff, 1987; Konovsky, Jaster, & McDonald, 1989; Womack, 1988), which labels the five styles as competing, collaborating, compromising, avoiding, and accommodating. The Rahim Organizational Conflict Inventory–II provides another example (Rahim, 1983; see also Hammock, Richardson, Pilkington, & Utley, 1990; Weider-Hatfield, 1988). Rahim labels the five styles as dominating, integrating, compromising, avoiding, and obliging. Table 2.1 reports four items for each style. These items were selected because they obtained the highest loadings in Rahim's (1983) study.

Some self-report measures are used to infer ability or skill in managing conflict situations. Covey and Dengerink (1984), for instance, created the Relational Behaviors Survey (RBS) to assess individuals' ability to successfully resolve conflict in heterosocial dating relation-

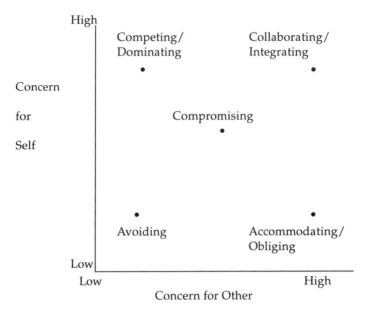

Figure 2.1. Styles of Managing Interpersonal Conflict
SOURCE: Adapted from Kilmann & Thomas (1977) and Rahim (1983).

ships. The RBS consists of 43 hypothetical conflict situations and five response alternatives for each situation. For each situation, respondents indicate which response alternative best describes their actual or probable response. Responses are scored from 0 (least effective) to 4 (most effective), employing norms previously established in the same population (using the behavioral analytic method, Goldfried & D'Zurilla, 1969). The following presents an example situation. Coding scores are in parentheses before each response alternative (Covey & Dengerink, 1984, p. 327):

> Example: You have not called your partner for some time. Your partner calls you and scolds you for failing to call. You begin to argue. In this situation, I would:
>
> (3) a. Tell my partner to call me if I don't call him or her
>
> (0) b. Hang up
>
> (1) c. Tell my partner that I will call when I have a reason
>
> (4) d. Promise to call more often
>
> (2) e. Tell my partner that I've been too busy to call

Table 2.1 Example Items From Rahim's (1983) Organizational Conflict
Inventory

Integrating

    6. I try to work with my _____ to find solutions to a problem
which satisfy our expectations.

  15. I exchange accurate information with my _____ to solve a
problem together.

  28. I try to bring all our concerns out in the open so that the issues
can be resolved in the best possible way.

  35. I try to work with my _____ for a proper understanding
of a problem.

Avoiding

    3. I attempt to avoid being "put on the spot" and try to keep
my conflict with my _____ to myself.

    7. I usually avoid open discussion of my differences with my _____.

  22. I try to stay away from disagreement with my _____.

  32. I try to keep my disagreement with my _____ to myself in order
to avoid hard feelings.

Dominating

  10. I use my influence to get my ideas accepted.

  11. I use my authority to make a decision in my favor.

  24. I use my expertise to make a decision in my favor.

  31. I sometimes use my power to win a competitive situation.

Obliging

    2. I generally try to satisfy the needs of my _____.

  12. I usually accommodate the wishes of my _____.

  13. I give in to some of the wishes of my _____.

  30. I try to satisfy the expectations of my _____.

Compromising

    9. I try to find a middle course to resolve an impasse.

  20. I usually propose a middle ground for breaking deadlocks.

  21. I negotiate with my _____ so that a compromise can be reached.

  26. I use "give and take" so that a compromise can be made.

SOURCE: Selected items from Rahim (1983, pp. 371-372). Reprinted by permission
of Afzul Rahim and *Academy of Management Journal*.
NOTE: The word *boss, subordinates,* or *peers* appear in each blank space on different
forms of the instrument. Numbers to the left of the item indicate placement on the
original form. The items reported are those with the highest factor loadings for each
style as reported in Rahim (1983).

As indicated in the previous chapter, the universe of behaviors that can be exhibited during conflict is large. Furthermore, different instruments are designed to tap different features or types of conflict.

Straus (1979) developed the Conflict Tactics Scales (CTS) to assess conflict and violence tendencies within families. The CTS contains a list of behaviors for each of eight nuclear family role relationships (i.e., husband-to-wife, wife-to-husband, father-to-child, child-to-father, mother-to-child, child-to-mother, child-to-sibling, and sibling-to-child). Items tap three modes of dealing with conflict that are central to a "catharsis theory" of violence control. These modes include (using illustrative items from the husband form "A"): *Reasoning* (e.g., "I tried to discuss the issue relatively calmly," "Got information to back up my side of things"); *Verbal aggression* (e.g., "Yelled and/or insulted," "Threw something [but not at my wife] or smashed something"); and *Violence* (e.g., "Threatened to hit or throw something at her," "Pushed, grabbed, or shoved her"). The items include response categories that identify "the number of times each action occurred during the past year, ranging from 'Never' to 'More than 20 times' " (Straus, 1979, p. 78).

In addition to measuring conflict styles and tendencies in certain relationships, researchers assess perceptions of conflict behavior associated with a specific, recalled conflict episode. As indicated in Chapter 1, a common conceptualization groups conflict tactics into the three strategies of integration, distribution, and avoidance. These strategies have emerged in several empirical studies (e.g., Bell & Blakeney, 1977; Putnam & Wilson, 1982; Ross & DeWine, 1988; Sillars, Coletti, Parry, & Rogers, 1982) and correspond to Horney's (1945) distinction that human behavior reflects one of three orientations: moving toward others, moving against others, or moving away from others. An operationalization of these dimensions is provided by a scale developed by Cupach (1982) and refined by Canary, Cunningham, and Cody (1988). In addition to the category of integrative tactics, factor analysis by Canary et al. revealed subcategories of the distributive (i.e., personal criticism, showing anger, and sarcasm) and avoidance (i.e., topic shifting, semantic focus, and overt denial) tactics. Items representing these three tactics are displayed in Table 2.2.

Attitudes and Beliefs Regarding Conflict. Although they are often used as a proxy for overt behavior, self-reports are particularly well suited to measuring participants' (a) attitudes about conflict in general, (b) attributions and feelings about a particular episode of conflict, and (c) meanings and motives ascribed to conflict behavior (both self and other's behavior).

Attitudes in the recent past have been viewed as predispositions to behavior, and they are routinely assessed by self-reports. Some aspects of personality are reflected in attitudes that specifically influence conflict behavior. Brown et al. (1981; Yelsma, 1981), for example, developed a theory about how six personality factors predispose individuals to manage conflicts constructively or destructively. Brown and colleagues developed an instrument to assess these factors, which include the following: range of feelings, task energy, respect for community, respect for others, desire for control, and desire for one's own self-uniqueness. Each of these predispositions presumably contributes positively to conflict management. The sum score for all six scales represents an index of an individual's propensity to handle conflict constructively.

Some belief measures more directly and more obviously focus on conflict orientations per se. Researchers have constructed items that assess fundamental beliefs about conflict, such as whether conflict should be avoided or confronted (Crohan, 1992; Fitzpatrick, 1988a) and whether or not disagreement is destructive to relationships (Eidelson & Epstein, 1982). Similarly, Jones and Gallois (1989; Honeycutt, Woods, & Fontenot, 1993) created a measure of conflict *rules*, that is, expectations about what behaviors are obligated, prohibited, or preferred (Shimanoff, 1980) during conflict discussions with a partner (e.g., "Listen to the other person," "Don't raise voice," "Should get to the point quickly").

Self-report measures are also employed to assess attributions about the causes of, and responsibility for, conflict issues. As indicated in Chapter 1, conflict attributions are associated with conflict management behaviors (e.g., Sillars, 1980a, 1980b; Witteman, 1988) and with relational quality (e.g., Fincham & Bradbury, 1987b). Attributional activity peaks during and following conflict episodes (Orvis, Kelley, & Butler, 1976; Sillars, 1981). Individuals make judgments regarding partner's intent, who is to blame for the conflict (self vs. partner), whether the conflict is due to dispositional or circumstantial factors, and whether or not the conflict issue is stable (ongoing) (Fincham & Bradbury, 1987a; Harvey et al., 1978; Sillars, 1981; Thomas & Pondy,

Table 2.2 Episode-Specific Conflict Tactics

Integrative

I sought a mutually beneficial solution.

I reasoned with him or her in a give-and-take manner.

I tried to understand him or her.

I was sympathetic to his or her position.

I compromised with him or her.

Topic Shifting

I avoided the issue.

I ignored the issue.

I changed the topic of discussion.

I tried to change the subject.

Personal Criticism

I criticized an aspect of his or her personality.

I blamed him or her for causing the conflict.

I criticized his or her behavior.

I told him or her how to behave in the future.

Showing Anger

I shouted at him or her.

I showed that I lost my temper.

I was hostile.

I calmly discussed the issue. (reverse scored)

Sarcasm

I tried to intimidate him or her.

I used threats.

I was sarcastic in my use of humor.

I teased him or her.

Semantic Focus

I focused on the meaning of the words more than the conflict issue.

I avoided the issue by focusing on *how* we were arguing instead of what we were arguing about.

Overt Denial

I explained why there was no problem at all.

I denied that there was any problem or conflict.

SOURCE: From Canary et al. (1988). Reprinted by permission of the authors.

1977). For example, Fincham and Bradbury's (1992) Relationship Attribution Measure (RAM) assesses attributions for hypothetical problematic events (e.g., "Your husband criticizes something you say"). Participants indicate the extent to which they (dis)agree with six items that assess internality, stability, globality, intentionality, selfishness, and blameworthiness.

Finally, a host of perceived features of the conflict situation itself can be obtained by self-reports. These characteristics include such factors as the perceived frequency, intensity, and importance of the conflict, as well as subjective outcomes such as degree of resolution, satisfaction with the outcome, satisfaction with the partner, and so on.

Advantages of Self-Report Measures

Perhaps the chief benefit of self-report measures is that they offer the most direct estimate of how people *experience* interpersonal conflicts. These experiences moderately associate with the overt behaviors observed by researchers. Indeed, it is of theoretical interest how internal states (cognitions, feelings) of relational partners, which by nature cannot be directly observed, are associated with overt behavior.

Although self-reports do not provide an objective measure of actual behavior in conflict episodes, they do offer a meaningful appraisal of how people interpret actions. Conflict episodes are embedded within the larger relational culture—"a system of rules, roles, norms, rituals, expectations, and interpretive filters" (Metts, Sprecher, & Cupach, 1991, p. 170). Self-reports present "an ideal vehicle for gaining access to relational cultures and the meanings ascribed to the events occurring within those subjective worlds" (Metts et al., 1991, p. 170).

Another advantage of self-reports is that they can maximize the ecological validity of data. Conflict in close relationships often occurs privately and unpredictably. Self-reports can depict behaviors that occur naturally in the context of everyday mundane interaction—behaviors to which the researcher is not privy otherwise. Indeed, the most intense and belligerent conflicts are not observed directly by researchers, nor can they be induced without incurring ethical problems. Thus, self-reports offer inside information about real activities, compensating for the sometimes contrived or artificial flavor attendant on the situations that researchers can directly observe.

From a pragmatic standpoint, self-reports of conflict offer efficient data collection and analysis. Proper validation of carefully developed self-report instruments requires considerable effort. However, the resources needed to produce and evaluate meaningful data are not nearly as taxing as those needed for most observational schemes.

Disadvantages of Self-Report Measures

One significant limitation of self-report data concerns humans' perceptual biases and distortions. Retrospective recall of events is subject to the vagaries of memory and to the motives of impression management. The type of information recalled occurs in the form of Gestalt images and impressions, rather than accurate and objective details of interaction. Thus, self-report data are less likely to reflect precise frequencies of behaviors as much as the presence or absence of behaviors (Benoit & Benoit, 1988). Moreover, the emotional arousal associated with conflict in particular can impair an individual's ability to remember events accurately and judge behaviors fairly (Sillars, 1985; Sillars & Scott, 1983).

The type of information elicited by the researcher partly functions to distort self-reports of behavior. Individuals can access and report information more accurately when it pertains to events that are relatively specific, objective, and recent in time (Ericsson & Simon, 1980). Potential threats to validity increase, however, as the self-reported information pertains more to general observations and/or to events removed in time.

Several systematic perceptual biases also can contaminate the validity of self-reports. For example, the fundamental attribution error, whereby individuals tend to exaggerate the effects of personality when explaining the behavior of others and to inflate the effects of situation when explaining one's own behavior, is exacerbated during conflict (Sillars, 1981, 1985). Moreover, as conflicts become more intense and emotionally charged, individuals may be particularly susceptible to the negativity effect, that is, affording greater disproportionate weight to negative information in making judgments (Canary & Spitzberg, 1990; Sillars et al., 1984).

Self-reports also can exhibit a social desirability response bias. Individuals tend to want to appear "normal" and socially appropriate

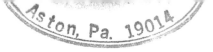

in their behavior, rather than abnormal and deviant. Some individuals may be reluctant, for example, to admit fully the extent to which they have engaged in abusive or demeaning behavior during conflict.

Finally, self-report data cannot adequately capture processual features of interaction. Although global impressions and summative appraisals serve various research purposes, individuals simply cannot self-report as much detail about the unfolding of an interaction episode as that which can be derived from recordings of interaction. As Markman and Notarius (1987) noted, "Perhaps the most salient factor mandating observational research is the inability of interactants to describe the ongoing behavioral process, that is, contemporary patterns of interaction" (p. 331). Hence, self-reports tell us relatively little about the microstructure and process of communication. In addition, communicators are often unaware of the complex and interlocking sequential patterns of their interaction. Individuals tend to be more perceptually attuned to their own feelings and responses and less aware of their partner's (Christensen, Sullaway, & King, 1983). In short, participants in an interaction lack sufficient systemic perspective to accurately portray dyadic, temporal patterns of communication.

Despite these limitations, self-reports provide valuable information about interpersonal conflicts. Their value is enhanced, of course, when used in conjunction with observations of behavior. The following section discusses issues relevant to observational analyses of interpersonal conflict.

❧ Observational Procedures

Observational analyses provide very precise, relatively objective, microscopic data that can be used in two ways (Gottman, 1979, 1994; Markman & Notarius, 1987; Weiss & Summers, 1983). First, observational codes can be aggregated. Such aggregates (or frequencies) provide a measure of participants' overall conflict behavior. Second, if each code represents a discrete point in the conversation (vs. overall judgment of use), then the codes can be used for sequential analyses. With such data, conflict sequences can be represented in such procedures as lag sequential analysis, Markov analysis, log linear analysis, and the like.

To obtain interaction data, researchers typically require participants to discuss topics designed to yield some conflict-relevant interaction. Couples discuss issues about which they in fact disagree (as in the "revealed difference" paradigm; Strodbeck, 1951), topics that previous studies have reported as problematic (e.g., sharing household tasks, showing affection, etc.; Gottman, 1979), or scenarios that the researcher, to increase disagreement, alters to bias each spouse (Olson & Ryder, 1970). Researchers may include a warm-up session wherein couples engage in small talk (e.g., about the events of the day). Although such conversations are not often considered conflictual, negative reactions sometimes occur here and are considered a form of relational conflict (Gottman, 1994; Notarius, Markman, & Gottman, 1983). Conversations last anywhere between 10 and 60 minutes, and these are usually preceded and/or followed by a questionnaire session designed to measure related variables.

The unit of behavior for coding is often the thought turn (or semantic turn), in which a change in semantical content indicates a different message requiring a code (Notarius et al., 1983; Sillars, 1986). Changes in thoughts can occur within speaker turns as well as between speaker turns, almost regardless of speaker turn length. "Punctuating" the interactions in this manner yields an impressive amount of data, because multiple thought turns often occur within turns and within a minute's time. Two popular alternatives to thought turns are small intervals of conversation (e.g., 30 seconds; Weiss, Hops, & Patterson, 1973) or speaker turns (Krokoff, Gottman, & Haas, 1989). According to one comparison (Hatfield & Weider-Hatfield, 1978), thought turns yield more reliable information. Once data are punctuated, coding commences.

Several methods for coding observed interaction behavior have been offered recently (for an excellent overview of interaction coding schemes in psychology, see Markman & Notarius, 1987). The most popular conflict coding schemes in psychology and communication have been the Marital Interaction Coding System (MICS) (Weiss et al., 1973) and Sillars's (1986) conflict coding system, respectively. We should note that the Couples Interaction Scoring System (CISS) developed by Gottman, Markman, and Notarius has received the most recent attention (Gottman, 1979; Notarius et al., 1983). Also, Patterson's Family Interaction Coding System (FICS) is the most widely used to assess interactions involving conduct-disordered children (Markman & Notarius, 1987).

Given their extensive use and operationalization of conflict, the content codes for the MICS–IV (presented in Table 2.3) and Sillars's system (presented in Table 2.4) are briefly discussed (for the MICS, see Weiss, 1993; Weiss & Summers, 1983; for Sillars's system, see Sillars, 1986; Sillars & Wilmot, 1994). At this point, we do not present the various decision rules nor the many applications of each scheme. We only wish to present them to underscore the kinds of behavior each emphasizes.

The MICS–IV (Weiss, 1993) provides a very flexible tool for coding couple interaction. The MICS–IV features nine higher-ordered functional categories for behaviors (problem description, blame, proposal for change, irrelevant, validation, invalidation, facilitation, withdrawal, and dysphoric affect), as well as codes for state of receiver (State Codes), forms of requests (Form Codes), and nonverbal affect. In addition, the individual codes can be grouped according to positive, negative, and neutral categories, although collapsing categories may entail a loss of predictiveness of specific actions (Revenstorf, Hahlweg, Schindler, & Vogel, 1984). For example, positive behaviors could involve the facilitation and validation codes, negative acts could include the blame and invalidation codes, and neutral messages would be indicated by problem description, proposal for change, and irrelevant codes (e.g., Vincent, Weiss, & Birchler, 1975). Unfortunately for generalization purposes, researchers have not been consistent in collapsing the codes into positive, negative, and neutral categories (Gottman, 1994; Weiss & Summers, 1983).

The MICS uses the thought unit and speaker turn as measures of observation. The coded data are analyzed at 30-second intervals. The individual or the couple serves as the unit of analysis, depending on one's research problem.

Sillars's system reflects two underlying dimensions. One is *engagement*, or the extent to which partners confront or avoid each other. The second dimension is *affect*, which references variations between friendliness and hostility. The presentation of the codes moves from indirect to direct message forms. In addition, the affect dimension separates confrontative remarks from those belonging in the conciliatory, analytic, irreverent, and noncommittal categories (Sillars, 1986). Un-

Table 2.3 Summary of Marital Interaction Coding System–IV (MICS–IV) Codes

---

State Codes

AT: Attention—listener maintains eye contact for 3 seconds

NT: Not Tracking—listener does not maintain eye contact for 3 seconds

Form Codes

CM: Command—direct request for immediate action fulfillable within the room in 10 seconds

CO: Compliance—fulfills command within 10 seconds of command

IN: Interrupt—listener breaks in and disrupts the flow of the other's speech

NC: Noncompliance—failure to fulfill command within 10 seconds

QU: Question—any interrogative statement, including rhetorical question

Nonverbal Carrier Codes

AS: Assent—listener says "yeah," nods head, or parrots to facilitate conversation

DA: Dysphoric Affect—affect communicating depression or sadness, any self-complaint or whiny voice tone

PP: Positive Physical Contact—any affectionate touch, hug, kiss, etc.

SL: Smile/Laugh—smile or laughter

TO: Turn-Off—nonverbal gestures that communicate disgust, displeasure, disapproval, or disagreement

VT: Voice Tone—indicates hostile or negative voice tone

WI: Withdrawal—broad category involving verbal and nonverbal behavior that implies that a partner is pulling back from the interaction

Defining Codes

A. Problem Description

PE: Problem Description External—a statement describing a problem that is external to both parties

PI: Problem Description Internal—a statement describing a problem that is internal to both parties

B. Blame

CR: Criticize—hostile statement of unambiguous dislike or disapproval of a specific behavior of the spouse. Nonneutral voice tone

MN: Mind Read Negative—statement of fact that assumes a negative mind-set or motivation of the partner

---

Table 2.3 Continued

PU:	Put Down—a verbal statement or nonverbal behavior that demeans or mocks the partner
TH:	Threat—a verbal or nonverbal threat of physical or emotional harm
VT:	Voice Tone (see above)

C. Proposal for Change

CS:	Compromise—a negotiation of a mutual exchange of behavior
NS:	Negative Solution—proposal for termination or decrease of some behavior
PS:	Positive Solution—proposal for initiation or increase of some behavior

D. Irrelevant

TA:	Talk—inaudible speech or "incomplete" speech units

E. Validation

AG:	Agree—statement of agreement with partner's opinion
AP:	Approve—statement that favors couple's or partner's attributions, actions, or statements
AR:	Accept Responsibility—statement that conveys that "I" or "we" are responsible for the problem
CO:	Compliance—fulfills command within 10 seconds

F. Invalidation

DG:	Disagree—statement or nonverbal gesture that indicates disagreement with spouse's opinion
DP:	Disapprove—neutral vocal tone
DR:	Deny Responsibility—statement that conveys "I" or "we" are not responsible for the problem
EX:	Excuse—denial of personal responsibility, based on implausible or weak rationale
IN:	Interrupt—partner breaks in or attempts to break in while other is speaking
NC:	Noncompliance—failure to fulfill command within 10 seconds
TO:	Turn Off—nonverbal gestures that indicate displeasure, disgust, or disapproval
WI:	Withdrawal (see above)

G. Facilitation

AS:	Assent (see above)
DE:	Disengage—a statement expressing the desire not to talk about a specific issue at that time. Neutral voice tone
EO:	Excuse Other—excusing partner's behavior or statement by providing a reason for that behavior or statement

continued

Table 2.3 Continued

HM: Humor—lighthearted humor; not sarcasm

MC: Metacommunication—statement that attempts to direct the flow of conversation

MP: Positive Mind Read—statement that implies favorable qualities of the other

QU: Question (see above)

PP: Positive Physical Contact (see above)

PR: Paraphrase/Reflection—statement that restates a preceding statement by the partner

SL: Smile/Laugh (see above)

H. Withdrawal

OT: Off Topic—comments irrelevant to the topic of discussion, including statements directed toward the experimenter, about the experimenter, or about the physical environment during the experiment

WI: Withdrawal (see above)

I. Dysphoric Affect

DA: Dysphoric Affect (see above)

SOURCE: Adapted from Weiss (1993) by permission of Robert Weiss.

like the MICS, Sillars's codes should not be grouped into positive, negative, and neutral categories, in the hope that the codes are not tautologically confused with outcomes, such as satisfaction or stability (Sillars, personal communication, 1994). Finally, Sillars uses the thought turn as the unit of observation, and the individual serves as the unit of analysis.

Comparing these two coding schemes using a small sample of interaction illustrates each scheme and suggests minor differences between them. In the following example, we use the thought turn, because this mode of punctuation is more sensitive to within turn variation. In the following example (taken from one of our data sets), MICS–IV codes are presented first, followed by Sillars's codes. As a courtesy, a coder at the Oregon Marital Studies Program, directed by Robert Weiss, coded this illustration using MICS–IV. (One of the authors applied Sillars's codes.) The issue under discussion is the extent to which the couple disagrees about how to spend their leisure time.

Turn	Message	(MICS–IV)	(Sillars's)
1.1	W: Sometimes we argue about what to watch on TV.	(PI)	(DES)
1.2	But it's not like we have a full fight.	(DR)	(EV)
2.0	M: Yeah, but you get mad when I flip the channels.	(MN)	(CR)
3.0	W: Yeah, but that's rude, 'cuz when you're in the middle of watching a show . . .	(DP)(TA)	(CR)
4.0	M: (interrupting) Yeah, but we're not watching a show, we're just messing around.	(PI)	(DEN)
5.0	W: But that, that's rude!	(CR)	(CR)
6.1	M: Oh, "it's rude" [sarcastically].	(PU)	(HJ)
.2	You should just say that instead of yelling.	(PS)	(HI)
.3	That's YOUR problem.	(DR)	(DR)
	W: (laughing)	(SL)	(UC)
.4	M: You gotta just TALK, and not yell!	(PS)(NS)	(HI)
7.0	W: Well, I did tell you that time.	(PI)	(DEN)
8.0	M: Nah, you're moody.	(MN)	(RE)
9.1	W: Well [in disgust].	(TA/TO)	(UC)
.2	OK	(AS)	(UC)
.3	[reads next question]	(QU/OT)	(PR)

In this example, the coding schemes present the same general picture. Both reflect a high frequency of negative behaviors. Both also reveal a chain of six negative lags, beginning at turn 3, where the woman reciprocates the man's criticism. This is followed by an excuse (denial) in turn 4, another criticism (turn 5), then a string of put-downs (or hostile joking and imperatives) by the man in turn 6. In turn 7, the woman denies the basis of his claim with an example, for which she receives prescriptions for future behavior (or hostile imperatives) in turn 8.

Table 2.4 Summary of Sillars's Conflict Coding System (Revised Version)

Denial and Equivocation (DE)

DEN: Direct Denial—statements that deny a conflict is present

ID: Implicit Denial—statements that imply denial by providing a rationale for a denial statement, although the denial is not explicit

EV: Evasive Remarks—failure to acknowledge or deny the presence of a conflict following a statement or inquiry about the conflict by the partner

Topic Management (TM)

TS: Topic Shifts—statements that terminate discussion of a conflict issue before each person has fully expressed an opinion or before the discussion has reached a sense of completion

TA: Topic Avoidance—statements that explicitly terminate discussion of a conflict issue before it has been fully discussed

Noncommittal Remarks (NR)

NS: Noncommittal Statements—statements that neither affirm nor deny the presence of conflict and that are not evasive replies or topic shifts

NQ: Noncommittal Questions—include unfocused questions, rephrasing the question given by the researcher, and conflict-irrelevant information

AB: Abstract Remarks—abstract principles, generalizations, or hypothetical statements

PC: Procedural Remarks—procedural statements that supplant discussion of conflict

Irreverent Remarks (IR)

JO: Friendly Joking—whenever there is friendly joking or laughter that is not at the expense of the other person

Analytic Remarks (AN)

DES: Descriptive Statements—nonevaluative statements about observable events related to conflict

DI: Disclosive Statements—nonevaluative statements about events related to conflict that the partner cannot observe, such as thoughts, feelings, intentions, etc.

QU: Qualifying Statements—statements that explicitly qualify the nature and extent of the conflict

SD: Soliciting Disclosure—nonhostile questions about events related to conflict that cannot be observed

SC: Soliciting Criticism—nonhostile questions soliciting criticism of self

---

Table 2.4 Continued

Confrontative Remarks (CF)

CR: Personal Criticism—remarks that directly criticize the personal characteristics or behaviors of the partner

RE: Rejection—statements in response to the partner's previous statements that imply personal antagonism toward the partner as well as disagreement

HI: Hostile Imperatives—requests, demands, arguments, threats, or other prescriptive statements that implicitly blame the partner and seek change in the partner's behavior

HJ: Hostile Jokes—joking, teasing, or sarcasm at the expense of the partner

HQ: Hostile Questions—directive or leading questions that fault the partner

PR: Presumptive Remarks—statements that attribute thoughts, feelings, and so on to the partner that the partner does not acknowledge

DR: Denial of Responsibility—statements that minimize or deny personal responsibility for the conflict

Conciliatory Remarks (CL)

SU: Supportive Remarks—statements that refer to understanding, acceptance, support, and so on for the partner and shared interests

CN: Concessions—statements that express a willingness to change, show flexibility, make concessions, or consider mutually acceptable solutions to conflicts

AR: Acceptance of Responsibility—statements that attribute responsibility for the conflict to self or both parties

Uncodable (UC)

SOURCE: Adapted from Sillars (1986) by permission of Alan Sillars.

Two subtle but significant differences in the schemes occur at turn 9. First, the woman's "well," which is delivered with displeasure, is double-coded as "talk" and "turn off" using the MICS but is less readily codable using Sillars's scheme (although one could code it as a form of rejection). The use of MICS extends the reciprocation of negative affect another turn. Second, the woman's reading of the next issue for discussion constitutes a topic shift according to Sillars's manual but is coded as assent using the MICS. Avoidance would be indicated by the MICS, however, if the videotape revealed that the woman was not tracking (i.e., removed eye contact) from the man during turn 8. However, given that these data were taken from tape-recorded conversations, we cannot offer any information about tracking behavior.

This example illustrates how Sillars's creation of indirect conflict types can reveal different forms of avoidance, which are not often specified in coding manuals. In addition, all the MICS codes can be grouped into higher-ordered positive or negative categories, whereas Sillars rejects this decision.

Advantages of Observational Approaches

Several strengths accompany microscopic observational coding. First, sequential analyses derived from observational data present specific probabilities of one code following another. In this manner, the researcher represents interactional processes of conflict, much of the time focusing on how behaviors might be reciprocated or might complement an alternative response. For example, Ting-Toomey (1983a), using a coding manual she derived from existing manuals such as the MICS, found that highly adjusted marital couples engaged in a pattern of coaxing, where lags 2, 4, and 5 obtained significant probabilities. For example, the wife might use humor and teasing, to which the husband (at lag 1) does not reciprocate the coaxing but uses any number of responses, none of which is significantly related to the wife's coaxing. At lag 2, the wife teases again, and again the probability of the husband reciprocating with humor is insignificant. After the wife teases at lag 4, the husband finally responds at lag 5 with humor of his own.

Second, sequential analyses appear to provide substantially more information than the baseline frequencies alone. For example, Margolin and Wampold (1981) highlighted examinations of discrete as well as grouped couples' conflict sequences, using the MICS. These authors confirmed previous findings that distressed (vs. nondistressed) couples engaged in significantly longer sequences of negative conflict (as in our example above). Margolin and Wampold also compared the relative contribution of sequential analyses over base-rate (aggregate) observations of conflict. They found between an 8%

and 15% increase in variance due to sequential analyses. In other words, more variance in satisfaction was provided by sequences than the simple frequencies of conflict behavior. This is impressive considering that the sequences correlated substantially with the base-rate frequencies.

Third, observations of conflict provide specific instances of couples' behavior, revealing precisely where positive and negative conflict occurs. Foster (1987) argued that intervention in particular conflict interactions requires molecular levels of observation. In other words, microscopic behaviors offer information needed to help people understand and manage their particular modes of communication exchange. But global, summary accounts of conflict do not permit such interventions.

Finally, observation of conflict interaction is less subject to indictments of perceptual distortion, social desirability, or common method variance when correlating reports of conflict to self-reported satisfaction or similar relational constructs. For example, a conflict item "I was cooperative" conforms to expectations for politeness. Clearly, agreeing with this is probably seen as more socially acceptable than disagreeing with it, regardless of what one actually did. Coders, however, are less susceptible to the actor's desire to be seen as socially acceptable.

Disadvantages of Observational Approaches

Observational methods for studying interpersonal conflict contain a few important drawbacks. The first regards the issues of face validity and criterion validity. Researchers often derive coding schemes that intentionally examine a wide range of interaction behaviors that can successfully discriminate satisfied from dissatisfied couples. As Resick et al. (1981) argued, "There is no evidence that these selected behaviors are actually components of the construct that the researchers are purporting to measure" (p. 59). Margolin (1990) indicates that although the MICS and CISS codes help discriminate distressed couples from nondistressed couples, "whether or not these are the most important behaviors is open to speculation" (p. 195).

To address the issue of face validity, Resick et al. (1981) conducted a two-phase study. They first obtained ratings of behaviors that discriminated hypothetical conflict from nonconflict interactions. They then observed couples' conversations about conflictual and nonconflictual issues. In sum, these authors found that four behaviors—volume of speech, criticism of the partner, disagreement with the partner, and sarcasm—differed between the two discussion types. In addition, the authors argued that rate of speech, gestures, and swearing (behaviors obtained from the hypothetical conflicts) were probably suppressed due to laboratory artifact.

The second drawback concerns a lack of ecological validity (Bronfenbrenner, 1979). Conflicts in the laboratory do not constitute "actual" conflicts, despite the fact that researchers do record actual conversations. Bronfenbrenner's comparison of laboratory and in situ interactions did not focus on conflict, and it stressed parent-child interactions. Yet his argument that roles and activities vary dramatically according to larger ecological systems appears compelling. For example, couples appear to enact fewer negative behaviors in the lab versus natural settings (e.g., Resick et al., 1981), although researchers have been impressed with the amount of negative behaviors couples do perform in the lab (Gottman, 1994; Weiss & Summers, 1983). Some of the artificiality of the discussion task can be alleviated by having couples participate at home.

Nevertheless, induced conversations about revealed differences or important relational problems are removed from the routines of daily life and involve unfamiliar modes of communicating (Weiss & Summers, 1983). As Sillars and Weisberg (1987) noted, conflict entails a "surprise element," insofar as partners do not anticipate or schedule conflicts in advance. Instead, as these authors argued,

> Conflicts hitchhike on other events. People have conflict over dinner, while on vacation, and when trying to get the kids off to school in the morning. Further, grievances are more likely to be felt when events in the situation are absorbing and stressful—for example, when the car repeatedly stalls or the checkbook doesn't balance—rather than during a lull in the interaction. (p. 157)

Unobtrusive (vs. laboratory) designs in the home, at work, or at the playground probably more closely resemble real conflicts (Vuchinich, 1987). Indeed, one research team sought to capture more realism by using the home as a "stage" for conflict. Margolin et al. (1989) sought to induce a sense of realism by videotaping couples as they reenacted a typical conflict in their home. Researchers followed the couples from room to room and probed them about what happened next. In a less obtrusive design, Krokoff et al. (1989) reviewed with couples in their homes how these couples manage conflict and then recorded their conflict-relevant discussions a week later.

Third, observational methods vary, a problem that is not unique to observational coding schemes (Markman & Notarius, 1987). Efforts to represent "objective" accounts—and (presumably) consistent re-cordings—of precise conflict interaction are countermanded by subtle and not-so-subtle differences in observational coding categories that naturally differ according to researcher perspective and purpose. In this vein, different use of particular codes works against synthesis. For example, Weiss and Summers (1983) presented a summary of findings concerning the MICS–III. Their summary table indicates that func-tional categories have not been consistently operationalized in the particular codes, a point Gottman (1994) and Hahlweg et al. (1984) also made. To illustrate, the negative solution (NS) in the MICS has been collapsed into positive, neutral, and negative categories, and it has even been excluded from such categories in the published litera-ture (Hahlweg et al., 1984). To complicate this issue, individual coding schemes are often revised as researchers fine-tune them. These incon-sistencies are due, in part, to improvements made through altering the codes. Likewise, Sillars's (1986) manual completely revised the higher-ordered functional categories that previously operationalized the integrative-distributive-avoidant typology to reflect better the two underlying dimensions of engagement and affect mentioned previously. Such developments are critical to the success of this kind of research. Still, the effort required to synthesize findings derived from the application of any one observational method (let alone more than one) rises in relation to its revision. And most schemes are revised over time.

A clear implication of the variation between and within coding systems concerns the amount of confidence one has in the present findings generated from any single coding scheme. One answer to this issue can be found by using more than one coding scheme, whereby researchers can compare the relative contribution of different conflict codes to predict relational stability (e.g., Gottman, 1994; Gottman & Krokoff, 1989). But given the next disadvantage, such an approach appears to ask too much.

A final drawback concerns how the specificity gained through observations of interactions costs time and money. Coding interaction data requires an incredible amount of time to train coders as well as to code the data. Notarius et al. (1983) noted that it takes a beginner of the CISS about 24 hours to code 1 hour of conversation and the more advanced coder requires 20 hours for each hour of conversation (Gottman & Krokoff, 1989). This means that an entire work week would be spent in coding only two couples' interactions. In addition, one must provide the equipment needed for analyses. This might include a laboratory and computer program materials to analyze the data, which Gottman (1987) estimates to cost about $30,000. These considerations led Weiss and Summers (1983) to recommend against clinicians using the MICS–III without technical support.

Coding Nonverbal Behaviors

Nonverbal communication behaviors reveal much about peoples' affective responses to conflict, perhaps more than verbal communication (Gottman, 1994). To underscore the importance of both verbal and nonverbal modes, Newton and Burgoon (1990a) concluded that an "adequate assessment of conflict behavior between intimate partners must involve both verbal and nonverbal behaviors" (p. 97). Given this supposition, it appears remarkable that so few efforts— relatively speaking—have focused on nonverbal behaviors. Three efforts have indicated why nonverbals during conflict merit a higher research priority.

Gottman (1979) reviewed some of the nonverbal research to support the inclusion of particular nonverbal codes in the CISS (see also Gottman's 1994 discussion). Gottman had coders rate interaction according to positive, negative, or neutral affect using nonverbal messages. For example, positive affect is indicated by a smile, head nods [yes], positive vocal features (e.g., warmth, caring, empathetic), and immediate body orientation (e.g., touching, open arms). Negative affect is indicated by frowns, sneers, vocal properties (e.g., tense, impatient, scared), and distant or withdrawn body orientation (e.g., hands thrown up in disgust, inattention). In addition, the nonverbal codes help researchers interpret the meaning of verbal codes; for example (according to the CISS), agreement accompanied by negative affect indicates sarcasm or disagreement. Gottman (1979) concluded that "the positive-negative dimension of nonverbal behavior thus discriminated distressed from nondistressed couples better than the positive-negative dimension of verbal behavior" (p. 108, emphasis deleted). Indeed, the inclusion of nonverbal affect codes in the CISS makes it comparatively advantageous to use (Markman & Notarius, 1987; Notarius et al., 1983).

Sillars et al. (1982) examined nonverbal correlates of five emotional states—reticence/talkativeness, affiliation, anxiety, deception, and reflectiveness. The following indicates the nonverbals that operationalized these affect states: *speech productivity*, as seen in average duration (in seconds) of speaking turns, average duration of talk per topic, average number of words per turn, and average number of words per topic; *speech hesitation*, as defined by pause time and inverse of speech rate; *illustrators* (number per 100 seconds); *adaptors* (number per 100 seconds); *eye glances* (number per 100 seconds); and *eye gaze*, or the percentage of time that eyes are fixed on partner. Using this scheme, Sillars et al. had undergraduates code nine different conversations involving roommate conflicts.

Sillars et al. found that speech productivity was associated positively with cooperative, integrative tactics; adaptors were more positively linked to avoidance than to integrative tactics; eye glances were negatively associated with integrative behaviors; and eye gaze was more positively associated with integrative than with avoidance and distributive tactics. Sillars et al. also explored how nonverbals predicted verbal messages. In short, being talkative best predicted cooperative conflict (followed by the negative predictors of adaptors, eye glances, and response time); distributive behaviors were also productively enacted but in "short bursts"; and there was no significant predictor of avoidance. Thus, at least in this study, cooperative (vs. competitive) conflict was marked by slower and longer speech duration, longer eye gazes, and less brief glances around.

Newton and Burgoon (1990a) argued that the midlevel (or mezzolevel) of observation—as contained in ratings of conflict—represents actors' interaction awareness and evaluations of partner behavior. In this study, four pairs of judges rated different dimensions of romantic couples' conversations (i.e., kinesic/proxemic vs. vocalics). Accordingly, 22 kinesic and proxemic indicators and 8 vocal properties were rated. The findings strongly supported the idea that nonverbals, more than verbals, affect relational message interpretations, communication satisfaction, and relational satisfaction. In particular, ratings of physical involvement and physical cooperation primarily affected relational factors (the latter were completed independently by couples following their conversation).

In sum, nonverbal affect is substantially associated with verbal conflict behaviors. Perhaps more critically, observations of nonverbals (vs. verbal messages) correlate more strongly with relational outcomes. Two implications arise from these observations. First, coding manuals should account for affect conveyed nonverbally, which then can be used for multiple purposes: (a) to interpret verbal messages, (b) to demarcate specific nonverbal messages linked to conflict orientations, and (c) to compare the relative effects of verbal and nonverbal messages. Second, it is clear that more observational research needs to be done on nonverbal features of conflict. We know relatively very little about nonverbal aspects of conflict interaction, although results provide evidence of its value for different research objectives.

Rating Processes: A Research Example

An alternative to coding each and every conflict behavior, whether verbal or nonverbal, would be to rely on rating systems that provide an assessment of the participants' overall methods of managing conflict-relevant interaction. This would substantially reduce coding time and expense. In addition, a researcher or counselor could use a more global rating system to find segments of interest that could be analyzed later using more microanalytic methods (Krokoff et al., 1989).

However, rating systems that have been used successfully also vary in their levels or units of observation. Consider the Rapid Couples Interaction Scoring System (RCISS; Krokoff et al., 1989) and the Interaction Behavior Code (IBC), a system applicable to parent-adolescent conversations (Prinz & Kent, 1978, reported in Robin & Foster, 1989). The RCISS requires that raters indicate at each speaker turn the positive or negative verbal and nonverbal code that represents that turn. Accordingly, the RCISS yields very specific information at about one fifth the time needed to use the CISS (Gottman & Krokoff, 1989). On the other hand, the IBC relies on overall impressions of the entire conversation and whether or not each of 7 positive and 22 negative behaviors was used. In brief, raters check a "yes" if the behavior was used and "no" if it was not used (Robin & Foster, 1989). Of course, rating schemes can fall between these two molecular and molar impressions.

For example, Margolin et al. (1989) rated reenacted conflicts in the home. Margolin and colleagues had physically aggressive, verbally abusive, withdrawing, and nondistressed/low conflict couples reconstruct typical conflicts step-by-step while being prompted for details and videotaped. These role-played conflicts were divided into thirds (regardless of their length), and each third was rated by a different assistant (ratings from 0 = not at all representative of person's behavior to 5 = highly representative). The three ratings were summed and grouped into the following seven categories (based on items derived through previous research, practice, and factor analysis):

1. *Overt Hostility:* attribution of problem to other, disapproval, anger, raising voice, badgering, and so on
2. *Patronizing:* condescending/patronizing, insensitivity, sarcasm, and so on
3. *Warmth:* playfulness, positive laughter, exhibit affection, and so on
4. *Problem Solve:* examine barriers to solution, generate solutions, cooperation, self-disclose, and so on
5. *Uninvolved:* cold/aloof, reluctance to talk, uninvolved
6. *Despair:* sad/depressed, sulk, hurt, and so on
7. *Defensive:* self-defense, disagreement, reject responsibility, and so on

Relying on the ratings of the videotapes, Margolin et al. (1989) found that physically aggressive couples were more overtly hostile and that physically aggressive husbands (vs. verbally abusive and withdrawn husbands) displayed increasing uninvolvement, defensiveness, and coldness. Nondistressed couples (vs. others) relied on more problem solving and warmth to manage their conflicts.

In discussing the methodological implications of their effort, Margolin and colleagues (1989) compared their procedure with microanalytic systems:

Microanalytic systems have the advantage of precision and reliability [though the rating scales were generally reliable], but often are at a disadvantage in terms of salience of individual codes or aggregated categories. Global systems, in contrast, generally are designed with the objective of theoretical significance. In meeting this objective, a larger burden is placed on the coders to aggregate frequency and intensity mentally into a judgment about the representativeness of each item. Thus, coding with a global system becomes a judgmental task requiring individual coders to make a holistic interpretation of the raw data. (p. 116)

One implication is that ratings become desirable when "holistic" interpretations of third parties sufficiently address the research issue. This appears to be the case when the purpose calls for aggregation of data or when relatively objective impressions of particular codes supplement conflict parties' impressions. In these instances, microscopic coding can be replaced by the easier and less costly method of rating.

❧ Conclusions

As we have seen in this chapter, survey and observational methods for examining conflict implicate many behaviors. Surprisingly, there are very few survey methods that directly examine conflict interaction. Many survey approaches focus on conflict-relevant factors, such as attributions, aggression, or relational problems not limited to conflict interactions. To assess interpersonal conflict behaviors, more observational systems have been offered. However, as noted, the selection of particular behavioral codes depends largely on the researchers' perspective on the topic, and some authors question these schemes' face validity.

A critical assumption that qualifies behavior as conflict interaction goes something like this: When couples discuss actual conflict issues or potentially problematic issues, they are engaging in actual conflict interaction. Although laboratory studies do yield some conflict behaviors, the assumption that *all* behaviors enacted during such discussions qualify as conflict behaviors is not sound. These discussions are abstracted from routines and the manner in which conflict unfolds, and they are constrained by experimenter demands and time limits. Real conflicts develop over days, weeks, and months, and they unfold when the couple is doing some activity besides talking about issues that others want them to consider.

Despite this criticism, observational methods provide the most concrete information about conflict interaction behavior. Patterns of interaction that cannot be detected or recalled by participants can be revealed through observational analysis. In addition, we should note that ethical constraints preclude researchers from ever observing actual conflict interaction as it emerges and progresses in real-life situations. Indeed, asking couples to reexperience conflicts through discussion or role playing can easily risk their emotional and relational welfare, especially if certain safeguards are not taken (e.g., instructing them to cease discussion if it becomes too heated).

It is no surprise that operational definitions of conflict vary. In many ways this reflects the diversity of definitions and conceptualizations. Still, more work needs to be done to link verbal and nonverbal conflict management behaviors together, using both survey and observational methods. Self-report and observational methods combined allow important comparisons and connections and afford some opportunities to triangulate observations about conflict behavior.

For example, Prinz, Foster, Kent, and O'Leary (1979) combined survey and observational rating methods to discriminate clinical from nonclinical families. Mothers and their adolescent children completed the Conflict Behavior Questionnaire, which assesses complaints about the other person as well as interactions between the two parties. They also completed measures concerned with the number of issues under disagreement, parental control, decision-making power, and mothers' day-to-day reports of conflict. The parent-adolescent pairs engaged in 10-minute conversations concerning an issue of concern to the adolescent. These were rated using the IBC's positive and negative codes. Prinz et al. (1979) found that more than 97% of the couples could be discriminated using a combination of self-report and observational methods. Mothers' reports of adolescent conflict and of dyadic conflict were the most powerful predictors. These were complemented by ratings of both parties' friendliness and adolescent negativity during discussion. Prinz et al. concluded that *both* the questionnaire and observation of behavior were required to make the most accurate predictions.

3

Parent-Child Conflict

This chapter is the first of three that examines research on conflict in types of close relationships. Congruent with our assumption that understanding interpersonal conflict requires attention to issues relevant to particular relational forms, this chapter focuses on theory and research concerned almost exclusively with parent-child relationships. More precisely, the parent-child relationship represents an involuntary association, an imbalance of power and resources, and an obligation for the parent to function as caregiver. These features, combined with a marked focus on development of the child, separate research on parent-child conflict from research concerning other relational types.

A primary theoretical issue germane to parent-child research in general concerns the direction of influence. Stafford and Bayer (1993) noted three causal alternatives. The *unidirectional* approach focuses on how parental behavior affects children. In this view, conflict is seen as the child's noncompliance to parental control. This view qualifies most as the one that lends practical credentials to the study of conflict, insofar as parents' behavior can be modified to increase parenting effectiveness. The *bidirectional* approach emphasizes how children influence parents as well and how both parties influence each other. The third approach emphasizes the *spiral of recursive feedback loops* according to system properties of parent-child interaction.

Most researchers of parent-child conflict adopt one of the latter two views, although some researchers still enter the dialogue by referencing noncompliance and parental control literature (e.g., Osborne & Fincham, 1994). Replacing examinations of child noncompliance to parental control (and its predominant unidirectional focus) with bidirectional views on parent-child conflict frees researchers from several constraints.

First, researchers are freed from the assumption that parents can enact effective conflict behaviors on a unilateral basis. This assumption is clearly questioned by research suggesting that effectiveness of unilaterally applied conflict strategies declines in conflicts involving adolescents (e.g., Prinz et al., 1979). Second, focusing on parent-child interaction as mutual influence permits a shift from framing conflict solely as a socialization process to understanding it as central to relational development between parents and children (Dunn & Slomkowski, 1992). Third, more productive outcomes can be explored, as Eisenberg (1992) indicated, "Focussing on noncompliance overestimates the destructive, unpleasant aspects of conflict" (p. 35). Finally, researchers can explore how conflicts emerge and are managed as important social phenomena independent of compliance attempts and outcomes.

For example, Patterson (1979, 1982) refuted the idea that parents can control their child's coercive behaviors through traditional applications of learning principles. For instance, positive or negative reinforcement may not promote desired behaviors or eliminate negative behaviors, such as noncompliance. Patterson extended social learning theory in viewing child coercion as a response to parental aversiveness. In other words, child coercion is conceptualized not merely as a response but rather as a mediating factor that functions as a punishment for parental neglect or other parental aversiveness. Patterson (1979) showed how parents' punishment of the child's coercion (e.g., whining, yelling, hitting, arguing) actually *increases* the likelihood that the child will continue using coercion. However, children using some forms of coercion (such as the child showing disapproval and ignoring the parent) were effective more than 50% of the time in eliminating the parents' aversive behaviors. Patterson's theory of coercive control implies that parents must learn how to adjust to the child's behavior, not vice versa.

Our discussion of parent-child conflict briefly provides a developmental context that frames much of the research. Next, we present the topography of parent-child conflict, which reveals the frequency of and topics about which parents and their children fight. We then discuss some conflict strategies and sequences. As we indicated in Chapter 1, how parents and their children manage conflict both affects and reflects the quality of their relationships. Next, we indicate some of the important positive and negative outcomes of parent-child conflict. Following that, we discuss how parents' relational problems, which culminate in separation and divorce, affect children.

⭐ Development of Strategic Interaction Skills

Parent-Toddler Conflict

At an early age, children display a working knowledge of rules concerning conflict, indicating an accelerated social learning curve. Children between the ages of 18 and 24 months also show high interest in conflicts between mother and a sibling (Dunn & Munn, 1985), suggesting this time frame as the initial period wherein toddlers indirectly learn social rules for managing conflict. Dunn and Slomkowski (1992) documented how by 3 years of age, children explicitly and differentially apply rules of positive justice to defend themselves, to obtain rewards, and/or to condemn culpable others. Their analysis showed that children enact behaviors that reflect maturity in use of social rules governing conflict, even before these toddlers can articulate the rules. Moreover, Dunn and Slomkowski noted that preschool children can sort the differences between moral versus conventional rules, contrary to what models of moral development might indicate.

Parents influence the child's conflict behaviors directly as well as indirectly. Lewis and Feiring (1981) charted how parents interact directly with the young child as well as indirectly. For example, a father's evaluation of the mother's performance might be communicated to the mother but not to the child, but that evaluation eventually affects the mother's interaction with the child. In addition, toddlers' observations of other family members (especially siblings) in conflict provide a rich resource to the child regarding how to manage conflict (Dunn & Munn, 1985).

Dunn and Slomkowski (1992) illustrated how mother-child conflicts become increasingly verbal (i.e., beyond a simple "no") as early as 18 months of age. For example, by 18 months, children learn how to tease a sibling by removing a desired object (toy or block), pulling the sibling's thumb from his or her mouth, and showing a rubber spider known to cause the sibling anxiety. Between 18 and 36 months, children's language skills develop dramatically. In comparing 18-, 24-, and 36-month-old toddler use of justifications in conflicts with mothers and peers, Dunn and Munn (1987) found that the total proportion of justifications increases from .04 at 18 months to .32 at 36 months. Importantly, children in this study showed that at 36 months they understood that justifying destructive behavior is not persuasive. In her study of 4-year-olds, Eisenberg (1992) found that 36% of children's arguments involved justifications. In addition, Vaughn, Kopp, and Krakow (1984) revealed how one sample of 30-month-old children could "filibuster" against the mother's control attempts.

Increases in toddler use of justifications and appropriate application of different justifications follow the mother's increased and selective use of justifications beginning at about 18 months (Dunn & Munn, 1987; Eisenberg, 1992). Dunn and Munn (1985) observed that even mothers of 16-month-old toddlers provided explicit reference to social rules and to violations of these rules, whereas before this time mothers relied on such labels as "naughty" and "nice." Similarly, Kuczynski, Kochanska, Radke-Yarrow, and Girnius-Brown (1987) found that mothers increased their use of reasoning and bargaining between 18 and 36 months, while decreasing their use of distraction.

Researchers agree that mothers serve as the primary caregiver (Stafford & Bayer, 1993). Not surprisingly, then, mothers tend to participate in much more parent-child conflict than do fathers—according to Vuchinich (1987), twice the amount—which means that mothers tend to have more input into children's acquisition of conflict management skills.

Parent-Adolescent Conflict

During adolescence, sons become more influential and assertive at the expense of the mother but not of the father (Jacob, 1974). In other words, sons become more forceful over time and mothers tend to complement those control attempts by being less dominant, whereas fathers become more dominant with their sons (Paikoff & Brooks-Gunn, 1991). In addition, adolescents more than mothers (but not fathers) engage in justification as an argument strategy during conflict (Smetana, Braeges, & Yau, 1991). Of course, the irony is that parents—and, mostly mothers—spend thousands of hours teaching their young children how to manage conflict. Parents indicate to their young children social rules that serve as guidelines for appropriate action as well as variations on interpersonal strategies, such as reasoning and bargaining, which help enable the child to achieve important goals. It appears that once these interpersonal lessons are mastered, they can be used against the teacher, who most often is the mother.

What processes explain how physical changes due to puberty affect the family system? Paikoff and Brooks-Gunn (1991) presented three models of direct and indirect ways that puberty affects parent-child relationships through interaction: (a) direct links between physical features and interaction, (b) indirect links (e.g., by first affecting increased experience of negative emotions), and (c) effects that work in combination with other processes (e.g., changes in social cognitions). Figure 3.1 reports these three models.

Paikoff and Brooks-Gunn reviewed relevant research for these models, finding support for each. In model A, adolescent hormonal changes (e.g., increased androgens) affect parent-child interaction both directly and indirectly through emotional changes (such as increased aggression or depression) and behavioral changes (such as not cleaning as much as before).

In model B, puberty affects interaction in the form of secondary sex characteristics that indicate reproductive ability (e.g., breast budding). Here, the development of such characteristics, their early or late arrival, and their rate (i.e., slow vs. fast) may directly affect interaction. For example, Steinberg (1981) provided convincing evidence that physical changes in the male adolescent dramatically affect conflict interactions. In analyses that do not and then do control for chronological age, Steinberg and Hill (1978) assessed how male physical development was tied to conflict behaviors. For example, adolescent interruptions were negatively correlated with adolescents' age ($r = -.29$)

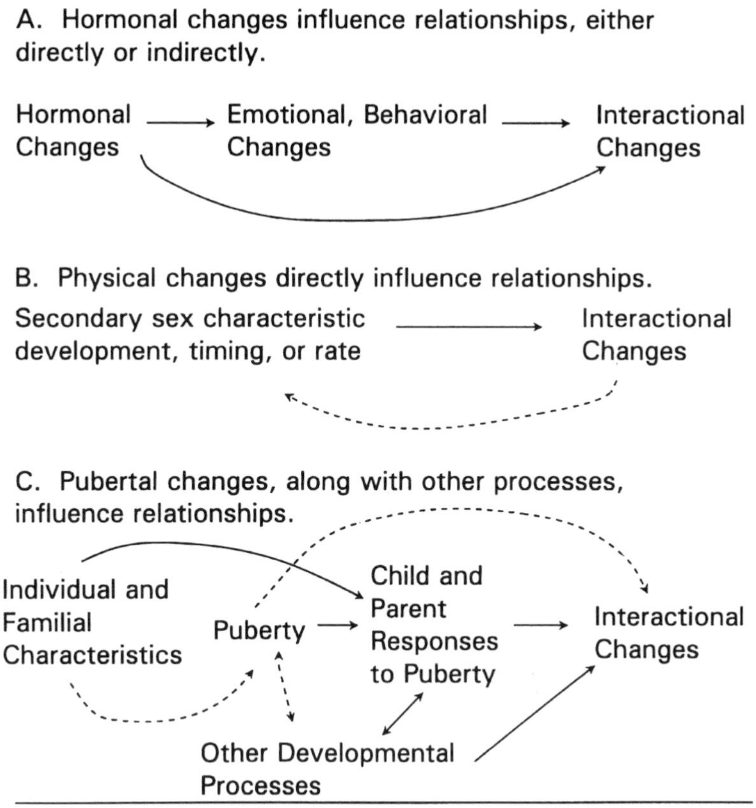

A. Hormonal changes influence relationships, either directly or indirectly.

Hormonal ⟶ Emotional, Behavioral ⟶ Interactional
Changes   Changes   Changes

B. Physical changes directly influence relationships.

Secondary sex characteristic ⟶ Interactional
development, timing, or rate   Changes

C. Pubertal changes, along with other processes, influence relationships.

Individual and   Child and
Familial   Puberty ⟶ Parent ⟶ Interactional
Characteristics   Responses   Changes
                                 to Puberty

Other Developmental
Processes

Figure 3.1. Three Models Referencing the Effect of Puberty on Parent-Adolescent Conflict

SOURCE: From Paikoff and Brooks-Gunn (1991). Copyright © 1991 by the American Psychological Association. Reprinted by permission of APA and Roberta Paikoff.

but were positively correlated with ratings of adolescent physical maturity ($r = .38$ for interruptions of fathers and $r = .40$ for interruptions of mothers). Similarly, adolescent explanations for his or her actions increased with age ($r = .60$) but decreased with adolescents' physical development ($r = -.70$). In other words, and when controlling for age, the more adolescents developed physically, the less they explained themselves to their parents. These correlations are all the more remarkable when one considers that chronological age and physical maturity were positively correlated.

Steinberg (1981) also observed that parent-child conflict was most frequent at the height of male puberty and only after late puberty (about age 18) did the conflict subside. Steinberg found that mothers defer to their sons in late puberty, whereas fathers become more assertive (and sons become more deferential). In addition, Steinberg found that, over time, sons become more influential than their mothers (but not their fathers) in family decision making. However, the findings of another study suggest that the relatively late physical maturity of males also allows sons to rebuff attempts by the father to control them (Comstock, 1994). More specifically, Comstock found that sons mirror their fathers' competitive behavior (but not the mothers') as the sons enter late adolescence.

Model C in Figure 3.1 indicates a complex interplay of social, cognitive, physical, and physiological factors that moderate the link between puberty and parent-child interaction (Paikoff & Brooks-Gunn, 1991). These factors include: (a) family responses to adolescent physical changes; (b) developmental processes, including adolescent development of social cognitive processes (e.g., attributions), parent as well as adolescent identity changes, and development of other social relationships; and (c) individual and family properties, such as ego control, ethnicity, and family structure.

For example, Paikoff and Brooks-Gunn noted how families may differ in their responses to puberty. One issue concerns how open families are to discussing puberty. Openness about physical changes during puberty appears to have a positive effect on how the child feels about him- or herself and on the parent-child relationship. However, some issues are seldom discussed (e.g., only 15% of daughters disclose the onset of menarche with their fathers; similarly, only 15% of sons discuss ejaculation) (Paikoff & Brooks-Gunn, 1991). They concluded that the withholding of information and feelings from parents about changes during puberty may lead to continued distancing and conflict. In short, Paikoff and Brooks-Gunn's review suggests that parent-child conflict stemming from issues surrounding child puberty are more complex than model A or model B reveal.

In an attempt to account for the most crucial factors surrounding parent-adolescent conflict, Robin and Foster (1989) merged social

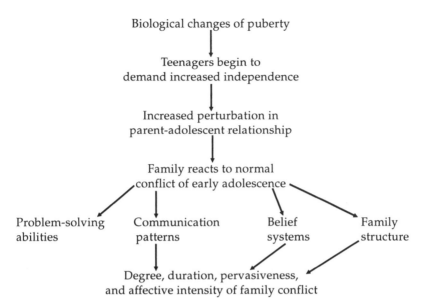

Figure 3.2. Robin and Foster's Model of Parent-Adolescent Conflict
SOURCE: From Foster and Robin (1988). Copyright © 1988 by Guilford
Publications. Reprinted by permission of Guilford and Sharon Foster.
NOTE: See also Robin and Foster (1989).

learning theory and systems theory. In particular, these authors focused on four components: (a) developmental factors in the adolescent, including biological changes during puberty and desire for
increased independence; (b) skills, including problem solving and
communication behaviors; (c) cognitions, including expectations of
upcoming actions, attributions of past actions, and irrational beliefs
that accompany conflict; and (d) structure of family relationships,
referencing such phenomena as alignments, coalitions, triangula-
tions, and degree of cohesion in the family. In terms of social learning
theory, conflict provides both positive and negative reinforcements to
behavior (Foster & Robin, 1988; Robin & Foster, 1989). Figure 3.2
presents Robin and Foster's causal process model.

As Figure 3.2 indicates, biological changes during early adolescence
trigger a desire for increased independence, which in turn results in
relational turbulence. Moreover, as Figure 3.2 shows, the family's
reaction to how the system changes is manifested in problem-solving

skills, communication patterns, beliefs, and family structure (e.g., coalitions and the like), which in turn affect the nature and intensity of family conflict.

Robin and Foster (1989, p. 32) offered five research assumptions derived from the model, for which they provided empirical support:

1. Because families are homeostatic systems, families engage in conflict in the face of disruptions caused by puberty and child independence to restore the system to homeostasis.
2. Deficits in problem-solving and communication skills during conflict lead to unresolved disagreements and unpleasant verbal arguments.
3. Adherence to unreasonable beliefs or misattributions about family life further exacerbates conflict.
4. Reciprocity of negative emotions is more prevalent in distressed families, whereas reciprocity of positive affect is less prevalent in distressed families (compared to nondistressed families).
5. Marital discord associates with parent-adolescent conflict "either when marital conflict is severe and long-standing or when adolescents' conflictual behavior comes to serve inappropriate homeostatic functions in parents' affairs."

This theory clearly stresses adolescent relationships. In addition, the connections between social learning theory and systems theory require fuller treatment than what we can offer here. Nevertheless, Robin and Foster's model and assumptions capture much research on parent-child conflict.

Puberty requires that both the parent and the child develop as individuals. Smetana (1988) argued that parent-adolescent relationships change because of two persons' development, not just one. Adolescents deal with the psychological peaks and valleys of puberty while their parents traverse middle age. Paikoff and Brooks-Gunn (1991) concluded that the "developmental task" for the adolescent "involves the acceptance of higher levels of reasoning about social conventions that results in enhanced perspective taking" (p. 57) and increased understanding of others' expectations for behavior; the parents' developmental task includes accepting the adolescent's desire for personal control and withholding the belief that the adolescent should follow their social conventions (see also Robin & Foster, 1989; Selman, 1980).

❧ The Topography of Parent-Child Conflict

Occurrence and Issues of Conflict

Shantz and Hartup (1992) argued that parent-child conflict is not limited to toddlers in their "terrible twos" or adolescent conflict; instead, family conflict is "developmentally relevant across the life span" (p. 6). Despite the cogency of this position, research has focused on young child or adolescent conflict, leaving the impression that once an adolescent graduates to adulthood, developmental processes become irrelevant—or at least less important—to how individuals manage conflict. Accordingly, existing research provides insights about individual growth and interpersonal conflict primarily in terms of toddlers and adolescents.

Dunn and Munn (1987) observed 2 hours of mother-child interactions involving 18-, 24-, and 36-month-old toddlers. They found that complex disputes, which refer to protracted and competitive oppositions, occurred about three times an hour (frequency range = 5.26 to 9.02 per 2 hours). Moreover, simple disputes, or single conflictual actions, occurred about four times an hour (frequency range = 8.28 to 9.48 per 2 hours). Dunn and Munn also found that disputes about propositions (i.e., factual disputes) did not occur often and that the highest number of disputes involved 2-year-olds.

In conversational conflicts involving 4-year-olds, Eisenberg (1992) reported an average of 10.2 conflicts (mean oppositional turn number was 3.0) during the average 37.2 minutes of conversation, an incredible reported rate of 1.4 conflicts every 5 minutes. Eisenberg concluded that such conflicts typically (a) were frequent but brief; (b) did not disrupt conversation; (c) did not lead to increased anger or distress; (d) involved negative emotions, if any, at the beginning of the opposition; (e) contained a reason or alternative proposal at the beginning of the opposition; (f) sometimes involved one member dropping the issue; and (g) most often concluded in a standoff (64%).

Vuchinich (1984) recorded family conversations during dinner, finding 1,156 oppositional interchanges in 64 recordings of 52 families. This translates to 18 disputes per dinner, most of which ended in a standoff. However, it appears that different oppositions may concern the same conflict issue. For example, consider the following dialogue, in which George wants Randy to eat a piece of pie (from Vuchinich, 1984):

(9) **George:** Here you go, Susan. Randy'll take a piece.
(10) **Randy:**   No, I don't want any.
(11) **George:** Yes he does.
(12) **Randy:**   I ate twice tonight.
(13) **George:** There's always room for Jell-O™.

Turn 11 counters the opposition in turn 10, which constitutes one dispute, and turn 13 counters turn 12, which indicates a second dispute. Yet it is clear from the text that both oppositions refer to the same conflict issue and episode.

Vuchinich (1987) found that conflicts at the dinner table lasted up to 24 turns, with most lasting about 5 turns—the probability of continuing a conflict to the next turn was .68. In addition, most of the conflicts terminated in a standoff (61%), with neither side acquiescing. Other conflicts terminated with submission (21%) or compromise (14.2%—usually the mother). In other words, there is approximately a two-thirds probability that conflicts will continue from turn to turn and will conclude without clear resolution. But these conflicts do not appear to bother family members nor involve very important issues.

Regarding adolescent conflict, Montemayor (1986) observed, "Good estimates of the frequency of arguments and disagreements between parents and adolescents in nonclinic families do not exist" (p. 18). Montemayor reported roughly two substantial arguments per week between adolescents and parents, usually mothers (plus another three conflicts with siblings). But another study using self-reported measures derived very different results. Laursen (1993) asked high school students (mean age = 16.7 years) about their previous day's conflicts. These students reported a mean of 7.36 conflicts (range = 0 to 39) in three different relationships (with females reporting more conflicts than did males), indicating a greater number of conflicts than Montemayor reported. Researchers have agreed that the general trend is for conflict interactions to increase until midadolescence (about age 15) and subside during late adolescence (e.g., Paikoff & Brooks-Gunn, 1991; Steinberg, 1981).

Perceived severity and the communicative management of conflict appear to be more important than the frequency of conflict in terms of conflict consequences (see below). Montemayor (1986) reported that 15% to 25% of parents complain about conflicts with their adolescents, and 21% of the adolescents experienced "tumultuous" growth marked by "many serious" conflicts with parents (p. 18). Prinz et al. (1979) used self-reports of conflict, assessments of self and other, and observers' ratings of positive and negative conflict behaviors in parent-adolescent conflicts. The authors found that frequency of conflict did not discriminate nondistressed from distressed families. Instead, Prinz et al. found that *how* the conflicts were managed (especially in terms of mother self-reports and observations of adolescent negativity and friendliness) discriminated these groups 97% of the time.

One important reason for the discrepancy between reports of conflicts involving toddlers and adolescents concerns different use of definitions, as we discussed in Chapter 1. Some researchers stress routine oppositions, whereas other researchers only focus on infrequent but significant disagreements. Examination of issues under conflict may help clarify the nature of conflict involving parents and their children.

Issues in Conflict

What issues preoccupy parents and young children during conflict? Child noncompliance represents only one issue involved in parent-child conflict. In fact, children most often comply with parental requests—for example, Lytton (1979) found that children comply with mother requests 65.6%, and with father requests 69.8%, of the time. Indeed, children may initiate conflict regardless of a parent's compliance attempt. According to Dunn and Munn (1985), children "frequently appeared to anticipate and unilaterally create conflict with the mother" (p. 486), indicating a more active role on the part of the child. Consider the following example from Dunn and Munn (p. 491), in which the child (18 months) pulls the mother's hair hard:

Mother: Don't pull my hair! Madam! Don't pull my hair. No. It's not nice to pull hair, is it?
Child: Hair.
Mother: Hair, yes, but you mustn't pull it, must you?
Child: Yes! [Smiles]

Mother: No! No!
Child:　No!
Mother: No. No. It's not kind to pull hair, is it?
Child:　Nice!
Mother: No, it isn't.
Child:　Nice!

Many issues appear to be at stake in parent-toddler conflict. Dunn and Munn (1987) reported the following problematic conflict issues involving 2-year-old children: caretaking, manners, rights, destruction of objects, aggression, rules of the house, physical space, and independence. Mother-child conflicts in this study mostly concerned child destruction and house rules (sibling conflicts mostly involved rights to behave a particular way). Using Dunn and Munn's categories, Eisenberg (1992) reported the following frequencies of conflict topics/issues between mothers and their 4-year-old children: possessions/rights (19%), rules or manners (15%), caretaking (11%), destructive/hurtful actions (8%), assistance (i.e., aid or interdependence) (6%), and other (40%). Consider the following example of a conflict about the child's rights, which concludes in a compromise earned through the mother's work:

Child:　[Approaching sister's day care] I'm gonna stay in the car.
Mother: Why don't you come in and hold my hand, okay?
Child:　Uh-uh.
Mother: There's no reason to wait out in the car.
Child:　[Whines] Well, I want to. So let me, okay?
Mother: Well, if you want to. Well, what about Tom and Emily? They're gonna wonder why you didn't come in. Do you wanna come and stand outside with them while I get Janie?
Child:　Yeah.

Eisenberg found that the parent's opposition to the child's requests for action and statements of intent led to more conflict than did child opposition to the parent's factual statements and requests for permission. This indicates that mothers permit a greater latitude of freedom and/or do not think the battle is worth the fight regarding relatively obvious kinds of statements (e.g., "The sun is bright today") and in terms of gaining permission.

Issues parents see as important, however, do provide occasion for conflict exchange. Dunn and Munn (1987) found that, in disputes concerning the child's rights (e.g., rights of possession, turns at play), mothers offered the most justifications and 3-year-olds showed the greatest anger and distress. It appears that such rights, especially concerning possessions, represent to the child the extent of his or her social control, an important issue for the child (Hay & Ross, 1982). Between 4.5 and 7 years of age, the importance attached to possessions and the rightful use of objects subsides and the importance of relational partner's actions (or lack of desired actions) and other's intrusive behaviors increases (Shantz, 1987). For example, children at about 5 years of age can become quite distressed when the mother will not play in a preferred manner. Such regulation of other's actions implies that the child desires social control and, through conflict, learns how to cooperate with others to achieve that control.

Inasmuch as control over his or her social world is important to the young child, control over his or her own activities and behaviors becomes preeminent to the adolescent. Naturally, however, the specific issues shaping control change. Smetana's research (1988, 1989; Smetana et al., 1991) has revealed the following conclusions about issues salient in parent-adolescent conflict:

1. The adolescent's view of the legitimate domain of parental control and supervision differs from the parent's view in two important areas: *personal* issues (such as sleeping in late on the weekend, talking on the phone, and "style" issues such as how to dress and how to wear one's hair), and *multifaceted* issues (issues that include any combination of personal/moral/conventional issues).

2. The adolescent and the parent agree about the extent of parental control in issues concerning *morals* (e.g., telling lies, stealing money) and *conventions* (e.g., doing chores, calling parents by their first names).

3. The adolescent and the parent do understand each other's perspective on justifications for their positions in conflict (e.g., adolescents state that parents see conflict as related to conventional and prudential/pragmatic outcomes, which is true). However,

4. The adolescent and the parent *reject* the legitimacy of the other's point of view. In other words, although they understand each other, they disagree about each other's right to presume that his or her own view has merit. Thus,

5. Parent-adolescent understanding of each other during conflict is less critical to productive conflict management than are developmental

changes that involve perspective taking. That is, conflict management leads to better outcomes if one ceases to persuade the other with regard to the "correct" attitude on the issue and instead abstracts oneself from the situation to understand the relational system in operation.

It is also clear from Smetana's research that adolescents reject some areas of parental control they once considered legitimate. On a more concrete level, Smetana, Yau, Restropo, and Braeges (1991) found the following issues as problematic: doing chores (20%), interpersonal relationships (16%), regulating activities (14%), homework and academic activities (10%), personality characteristics (8%), bedtime and curfew (8%), appearances (8%), regulating relationships (7%), money (5%), and health and hygiene (3%). These issues were equally problematic for married and divorced families with early or middle adolescents.

In summarizing issues at stake, Montemayor (1983) noticed two alternate features of parent-adolescent conflict. First, they are about routine, day-to-day activities, such as chores, schoolwork, and so on. Second, the issues remain the same across generations, indicating that today's "rebellious" adolescents mature into tomorrow's "controlling" parents.

As this research indicates, parent-child conflict involves more than child noncompliance to parental requests, although such conflicts do concern routine activities. The larger issue across developmental stages concerns the child's perception of his or her social control and, during adolescence, personal control. And these are not the only "larger" issues. For example, Emery (1992) argued that family conflicts can be cast as representations of underlying relational problems of power or intimacy. The dimensions of power and intimacy have been popular in the past as means to explain how interpersonal interactions reflect relational dimensions (Burgoon & Hale, 1984). Relational dimensions reflecting conflict may include other important factors, such as trust and commitment, as conflict between romantic partners has shown.

We now know that parent-child conflict operates in a bidirectional manner and that particular issues emerge as salient depending on the development of both the parent and the child. Unfortunately, researchers are silent with regard to conflicts involving parents and their adult children. We now consider the types of behavior that parents and children use during conflict.

Conflict Management Behaviors

Beyond conflict frequency and issues, the communicative management of conflict provides important information about the parties' view of their interaction and the relationship. As Comstock and Buller (1991) noted, "The valence assigned to conflict may stem from how people interact during conflict as well as the mere presence of conflict *per se*" (p. 57). As we noted in Chapter 1, there are diverse typologies of conflict behaviors, and research in parent-child conflict readily illustrates this observation. Nevertheless, conflict management behaviors can be distinguished along two continua: valence and engagement (Sillars & Wilmot, 1994). In other words, conflict interaction can be classified according to positivity versus negativity of conflict behaviors and direct versus indirect discussion of the issue.

Positive and direct conflict behaviors are represented in *integrative tactics* (Comstock & Buller, 1991), *reasoning* (Straus, 1979), *rational discussion* (Rosenthal, Demetriou, & Efklides, 1989), *supportive communication* (Alexander, 1973), and the like. Negative and direct conflict messages are displayed in such actions as *distributive tactics* (Comstock & Buller, 1991), *verbal aggression* (Straus, 1979), *emotional expression of hostility* (Rosenthal et al., 1989), and *defensive communication* (Alexander, 1973).

Indirect methods may reflect positive or negative forms. For example, to prevent a destructive escalation *or* to escape responsibility for one's actions, one might engage in *avoidance* (Comstock & Buller, 1991), *avoidance of confrontation* (Rosenthal et al., 1989), *distraction* (Vuchinich et al., 1988), *withdrawal* (Whittaker & Bry, 1991), and the like.

However, Sprey (1971) argued against the a priori grouping of conflict behaviors in positive and negative categories. Instead, Sprey held that "whether or not a given interchange between family members is to be seen as positive or negative should depend on its strategic appropriateness" (p. 725). We concur that, although it appears obvious, for most families, positive and direct integrative conflict behaviors are perceived as more competent than negative and direct distributive acts, which in turn appear less desirable than indirect avoidant behaviors (Canary & Cupach, 1988; Canary & Spitzberg, 1990).

In his summary of the literature, Montemayor (1986) noted that functional parent-adolescent dyads enact more positive than negative interactions, with a low probability of reciprocating negative messages. For example, Alexander (1973) compared interactions of families of delinquent children (runaways and "ungovernable" children) to those of families of nondelinquent children. Alexander relied on Gibb's (1961) notions of supportive and defensive communication. *Supportive communication* refers to giving and seeking genuine information, spontaneous problem solving, empathy, and equality, whereas *defensive communication* includes judgmental dogmatism, controlling and strategic behaviors, indifference, and superiority. Alexander found that delinquent families enacted more defensive communication within all dyad pairs, but only in child-to-parent messages did delinquent families exhibit lower levels of supportive communication.

Perhaps more intriguing is Alexander's finding that in normal families, parents and children reciprocated each others' supportive communication but not defensive communication. In contrast, family members with delinquent adolescents reciprocated some defensive communication but not supportive communication. In a related manner, and analyzing ratings of self-reported conflict strategies, Comstock and Buller (1991) found significant correlations between parent-adolescent conflict behaviors, providing some evidence of reciprocation during interaction. Interestingly, the correlations for parent-child distributive behaviors were only significant in conflicts regarding issues of lasting concern to the adolescent. The findings of the Alexander and Comstock and Buller studies are consistent with peer and marital communication research showing that dysfunctional dyads tend to reciprocate negative messages for longer periods of time than do functional dyads (e.g., Gottman, 1994; Sillars, 1980b; Ting-Toomey, 1983a).

In addition, we should note that the effectiveness of a particular strategy depends on its behavioral context—that is, what preceded the message. In other words, messages enacted during conflict occur within an ongoing stream of behavior and activities, not in isolation. For instance, Lytton (1979) found that actions immediately preceding a verbal strategy (i.e., within the previous 20 seconds) moderated the effectiveness of the strategy. For example, the use of physical control (e.g., holding down a child) just before a command-prohibition weakened the effectiveness of the message, but immediate prior use of positive actions (e.g., hugging, playing with child) increased the command's effectiveness. Although Lytton was primarily concerned with parental control techniques, conflict messages also probably vary in their impact given the immediate interaction context.

❧ Consequences of Conflict

In many respects, conflict consequences defy simple summary. Not only do participants react to each other, they also are affected by their own message choices (Canary & Cupach, 1988). In addition, emotional, cognitive, and behavioral responses are bound together in the same conflict experiences, with more intense conflicts resulting in an overlap of ongoing emotional, cognitive, and behavioral responses (e.g., Zillman, 1990). That is, one's negative reactions to the other person's behavior do not entirely subside before second and third sets of reactions follow (Zillman, 1990). Conflict can also entail short- or long-term effects, not only on the individuals but also on the relationship between the parties and, indirectly, on other interested members. Finally, conflict functions as most interaction functions, as a way for the relational system to perpetuate itself. Often during conflict, each relational system can reify what it values as normative and appropriate conduct. Comparing 1950s to 1990s prototypical TV families, for example, Ozzie and Harriet consistently approached problems with their adolescents in a calm, integrative manner, whereas Rosanne Arnold thrives on combative, threatening exchanges. Despite these caveats, several direct and indirect interaction consequences for the individual and the relationship have emerged.

Direct Consequences

First, conflict interactions between parent and child affect the development of both the child and the parent (e.g., Shantz & Hartup, 1992). For example, many theorists have postulated that social perspective taking skills are facilitated through conflict interaction (e.g., Paikoff & Brooks-Gunn, 1991; Selman, 1980). Children learn that, in order to obtain their own objectives, they need to understand the perspective of the opposing party and how conflict processes function. In addition, conflict interactions provide instances wherein parents learn how to negotiate beliefs, norms, and rules with their children.

Second, the child learns how to manage conflict directly from the parent (e.g., Minuchin, 1992). We noted previously that parent-child conflict involves reciprocation of messages, which indicates an immediate reinforcement of particular behaviors as appropriate. In systems terminology, Alexander (1973) concluded that normal families promote "parentlike" behaviors in children, recalibrating the system to adapt to adolescent moves toward independence. However, according to Alexander, deviant families do not recalibrate but, instead, enact destructive cycles that erode the family system.

Third, parent-child conflict can powerfully affect the child's personal and social adjustment. Montemayor's (1983) review indicated that parent-adolescent conflict is linked to troubled adolescence and specifically to drug use, self-esteem problems, and suicide. Examining intact and divorced families, Fauber, Forehand, Thomas, and Wierson (1990) found that the mother's rejection and withdrawal, especially among children of divorced parents, was most powerfully linked to child adjustment problems.

Fourth, daily interactions in neglectful or abusive families provide little support to the child. Research indicates that deviant families experience (a) less talk overall, (b) less equity in communication behaviors when they do talk to each other, (c) fewer positive interruptions, (d) more negativity toward each other, and (e) fewer shared activities (Burgess & Conger, 1978). Burgess and Conger found substantial differences between neglectful and normal families, with neglectful mothers particularly negative toward their children in terms of showing disdain and asking for more compliance from the child but ignoring the child's requests. Similarly, in a comparison of distressed versus nondistressed families, Prinz, Rosenblum, and O'Leary (1978) found that distressed mothers wrote and exhibited more negative behaviors. Distressed mothers complained more about disrespect, were more demanding, attacked the child verbally, and demonstrated anger—and their children exhibited similar destructive behaviors, including complaining about unfairness. Fortunately, the research indicates that most parents are not neglectful or abusive, and they manage conflict in more productive ways, which leads to the last point.

Fifth, for a majority of families, conflict has no long-term detrimental relational effects. For example, Laursen (1993) found that adolescents do engage in negative, dramatic conflict episodes but believe that the parent-child relationship can sustain more intense expressions of disagreement, especially in comparison to the effects reported for peer or marital involvements (cf. Montemayor, 1986). Paikoff and Brooks-Gunn (1991) reported that only 5% to 10% of families with adolescents experience a decline in parent-child relationships, indicating that parent-child conflicts "contribute in positive ways to adolescent development, through greater individuality in the context of a warm parental relationship" (p. 50). Eisenberg (1992) characterized mother-child conflicts as containing a small amount of negative affect (17.6%), which the children usually initiate at the beginning of the conflict. This suggests that conflict as oppositions involving young children are not emotionally intense melodramas as much as squabbles that last a few turns. Such squabbles do not have a serious effect on the relationship, although they likely result in some wear and tear on the child and (no doubt) on the parent as well.

Indirect Effects

As mentioned earlier, children are affected by parental interaction indirectly as well as directly. Lewis and Feiring (1981) discussed two types of indirect effects (where A and B refer to parents, and C refers to the child): (a) A-B-C interactions, in which A influences the B-C discussion but is absent from it; and (b) A-B-C interactions, where C observes the A-B conversation. Lewis and Feiring cited research support of how marital relations eventually affect the child in terms of modeling, inhibitory effects, and facilitating effects.

Minuchin (1992) noted how parents' lack of competence in managing conflict leads to parental neglect and abuse of the child. Moreover, Minuchin's review suggests that children of neglect learn the parents' avoidant conflict behaviors and children of abuse will, in the future, model the parents' destructive behaviors. Accordingly, conflict behaviors are likely modeled and learned within families.

How parents manage conflict between them can also critically affect the children's personal and social adjustment. Amato and Keith's (1991) meta-analysis revealed that children in high-conflict homes were less adjusted than were children in low-conflict homes *and* children of divorce. In addition, Amato and Keith found that children of divorce whose parents did not enact negative conflict behaviors were *better* adjusted than were children of divorce whose parents displayed negative conflict behaviors. Given the amount of attention paid to this issue, we briefly elaborate on how marital conflict affects children's adjustment.

First, children at a young age appear to respond quite negatively to adult conflict. Cummings and colleagues (e.g., Cummings, Iannotti, & Zahn-Waxler, 1985; Cummings, Zahn-Waxler, & Radke-Yarrow, 1984) have documented in natural and experimental settings that toddlers respond to adult expression of anger with distress, as indicated in the child's body posture, body movement, and sometimes in the child's face or in crying. In addition, although young children showed increased distress at a second display of adult anger, the overall pattern indicates that older children compensate for adult anger in more active and prosocial ways (e.g., by acting as caregivers), although these children may, in fact, experience negative arousal due to adult conflict. Cummings et al. (1985) concluded that although conflict is natural to relationships, "how much anger can be tolerated or experienced safely is unknown and clearly, at some point, it becomes a detrimental experience" (p. 506).

The second finding concerning parental conflict concerns the child's negative personal and social adjustment. Whittaker and Bry (1991) found that parents of clinic adolescents (i.e., youths with legal, school, or drug problems) engaged in substantially more overt conflicts *and* silence in a 10-minute conversation than did parents of nonclinic adolescents (11.25 vs. 4.0 conflicts). These findings suggest that parents who engage in frequent conflict interactions present ambiguous, inconsistent messages regarding appropriate mature behavior. Such inconsistent messages could deter childhood adjustment and socialization. However, as stressed before, the form of conflict probably moderates the effects due to conflict frequency. Jenkins and Smith (1991) found that hostile marital conflict was positively associated with child behavioral and emotional problems, more so than the mere frequency of disagreements between parents regarding child rearing or covert tensions. The authors concluded that "[hostile] conflict is the element in a disharmonious marriage which is most deleterious to children" (p. 805).

Third, children may "take on the symptom" to distract parents who fight. Robin and Foster (1989) viewed such actions as an "inappropriate homeostatic" function enacted to restore harmony. That is, children behave in extraordinary and sometimes harmful ways to alleviate the tensions at home and to restore the family system as it once was. Emery (1982) suggested that boys engage mostly in *under-controlled* behaviors (e.g., showing aggression, running away), whereas girls engage mostly in *overcontrolled* behaviors (e.g., withdrawal, extremely prosocial actions). Accordingly, boys show social dysfunctions more obviously than do girls, although both boys and girls enact behavioral dysfunctions indirectly tied to their parents' marital conflict.

Fourth, in relation to divorce or separation, the literature clearly shows that parental conflict (more so than divorce or separation) predicts child adjustment problems. Emery (1982) held that the content, process, and duration of marital conflict have "more detrimental effects on children than do other aspects" related to parental discord and divorce, calling it the "principal explanation" for childhood problems during marital separation (p. 313). Emery cited two reasons for his conclusion: (a) separation effects are short-term, whereas conflict effects are long-term; and (b) marital problems and separation reflect other life changes that married partners experience.

In a meta-analysis of 92 studies, Amato and Keith (1991) reported that 70% of the studies found that children from divorced families showed lower adjustment than did children in intact families. However, the effect sizes for family status on the various measures were small (*M* effect size = .14). This small effect size indicates that parents' marital status accounts for less than 1% of the variance in childhood adjustment. Amato and Keith reported that the largest effect size for adjustment was found in comparing high-conflict versus low-conflict families. Children in high-conflict families scored significantly lower on indexes of appropriate conduct, psychological adjustment, and self-concept than did children in low-conflict families. Overall, the high-conflict children were worse off than were divorced children in terms of psychological adjustment and self-esteem.

Finally, and crucially, it appears that direct interaction with the parent mediates indirect effects of the parents' marital conflict. For example, Hess and Camara (1979) found that positive relationships with both parents led to higher child adjustment in terms of less aggression, more social skills, and greater work productivity. Hess and Camara argued that the parents' relationship appears less important to the child than the child's direct relationship with the parents. Likewise, Fauber et al. (1990) found that the child's adjustment problems due to parental conflict were strongly mediated by the mother in terms of her psychological control, rejection/withdrawal behaviors, and degree of lax control (i.e., little supervision). In other words, when the parent (in this case the mother) presents herself as interested in the attitudes and activities of the child and does not reject or withdraw from the child, the child experiences fewer adjustment problems. In addition, positive parent-child relationships reduce the child's feelings of being caught "in the middle" between the parents in terms of the child's loyalty or love or as a negotiator of parental conflict (Buchanan, Maccoby, & Dornbusch, 1991).

In sum, research indicates both direct and indirect effects due to conflict. Research on direct effects shows (a) conflict is linked to the development of both the parent and the child, though research has (understandably) emphasized child development; (b) how children learn conflict management techniques; (c) neglectful or abusive family behaviors are often learned and thereby perpetuated; (d) parent-child conflict powerfully affects child adjustment; and (e) parent-child relationships tend to be remarkably resilient to negative long-term outcomes due to conflict. Research on indirect effects indicates (a) children, especially at a very young age, respond negatively to parental conflict; (b) hostile marital conflict negatively affects healthy internal and external behaviors (e.g., increased depression and antisocial behaviors); (c) children attempt to alleviate marital discord through their own actions; (d) conflict more than divorce affects child adjustment; but (e) the direct parent-child relationship dramatically reduces the potential negative indirect effects arising from parental conflict.

☙ Conclusions

Researchers have invested considerable energy in order to understand parent-child conflict. Several impressions can be gleaned from this literature.

We know much about the role of conflict in young child and adolescent development. The parent-child conflict literature shows how communication is incrementally and strategically used to achieve personal goals. Justifications first appear at about 18 months and become part of the child's repertoire by about 36 months. In addition, social perspective taking develops and sharpens through conflict. The family most often provides a safe environment wherein these conflict perceptions and management behaviors are learned, although a minority of families experience tumultuous periods of conflict. Mothers (more than fathers) tutor their children in the art of conflict management strategies, which is ironic given that mothers tend to lose social control to their adolescent sons. In addition, most family systems appear to recalibrate (i.e., adjust to changes during adolescence) by the time children become adults.

Conflicts involving parent-child interactions typically reflect the routines of daily living. Oppositions appear quite common, and several different oppositions can accompany a single conflict episode. During the child's early years, conflicts often concern possessions that symbolize the child's desire for social control; during adolescence, conflicts often concern lifestyle issues that symbolize the child's desire for personal control. Although both parents and children understand each other's positions, they often simply do not accept the legitimacy of those positions. We know very little about problematic issues faced by parents and their adult children.

Perhaps more important than frequency, how conflicts are managed reveals a (dys)functional parent-child relationship. The commonplace oppositions experienced while cooking or driving the car appear to be relatively benign, though they no doubt test one's stamina. As we will find in other relational contexts, reciprocation of negative emotions during conflict represents a dysfunctional relationship. Not only does the reciprocation of negative affect escalate the conflict, it also positively reinforces the use of negative distributive tactics, despite desires to eliminate such negative behaviors. However, hostile parent-child conflicts represent a minority of family interactions. Moreover, when hostile conflict episodes do erupt, they appear to have few long-term detrimental effects on the parent-child relationship, indicating that conflicts involving young children and adolescents tend to be enacted within a context of support.

Some parents, however, do express their discord to the detriment of the family and the children in particular. This is clearly illustrated in neglectful and abusive homes, in which the child's adjustment and proclivity toward functional conflict management behaviors decline. In addition, children become maladjusted in part due to their own direct interaction experiences with parents or due to the indirect effects of their parents engaging in combative marital conflict. Still, it appears that a positive relationship with parents mitigates against indirect effects due to conflict between the mother and father.

In terms of development, the focus on young children and adolescents is understandable, given the impressive social skill acquisitions and personal transitions identified with these age groups. Clearly, however, much more research should focus on adult parent-child relationships. Much of the literature we reviewed provides many research findings that can be replicated and extended in adult parent-child relationships. The time for such research concerning adult parent-child relationships in general has arrived (especially considering that a rather large cohort—the baby boomers of the 1950s—now have adult children of their own).

Finally, it appears that we need finer, microscopic analyses of interaction behaviors and patterns in order to reveal conflict processes. Montemayor (1986) stressed this with regard to parent-adolescent relationships: "Ultimately an understanding of parent-adolescent conflict requires an examination of *process*. Why are some relations between parents and adolescents characterized by conflict, although others are not? . . . Unfortunately, researchers interested in the parent-adolescent relationship have paid little attention to process" (p. 21). Of course, many researchers in parent-child conflict provide excellent examples that illustrate interactions. But such examples, though rich in anecdotal detail, cannot summarize the patterns that describe the give-and-take of parent-child conflict interaction.

4

Conflict in Friendship

As was true of the literature on parent-child conflict, scholars also have noted the importance of peer (e.g., friendship, sibling) conflict in human development (e.g., Erikson, 1959; Hartup, 1992; Piaget, 1932; Selman, 1980; Shantz, 1987; Sullivan, 1953). For example, Furman (1984) noted that positive peer relations are "as essential for healthy adaptation as positive parent-child relations" (p. 103).

Relationships with peers contribute to development in several specific ways. For example, Hartup (1983) asserted that childhood peer relationships are associated with social and emotional development. Stocker (1989) noted that peer relations help children learn social perspective taking as well as social problem-solving skills. Bukowski and Hoza (1989) illustrated the links between peer relationships and adjustment in children and adolescents, and, finally, Corsaro (1981) highlighted the importance of peer relationships to children's cognitive development with regard to friendships. Evidently, peer relationships are important facets of people's lives.

Conflict with peers differs from conflict with parents in several important ways, including types of offenses, reactions to offenses, use of punishment, use of apologies, number of offenses, and ending patterns (Youniss, 1980). In addition, because of status differences, conflict with peers (vs. parents) not only reflects alternative behaviors but is associated with development in different ways.

Before we delve into peer conflict, we should discuss who qualifies as a "peer." Peer relationships, in theory and research, constitute a variety of relationship types. For example, participants in peer studies include strangers of similar age (e.g., Gottman, 1983), classmates (e.g., Stocker, 1989), friends (e.g., Shantz, 1987), coworkers (Putnam, 1988), roommates (Sillars, 1980a, 1980b), and, in some cases, siblings (Nadelman & Begun, 1982). Though each of these role relationships involves potential conflict, our focus is on close relationships. In this chapter, we emphasize conflicts between friends. Friendships qualify as close because they are characterized by knowledge of the partner, interdependence, and inability to replace the relational partner, defining features noted in the Preface. Although we focus on friendship research primarily, relevant research from other areas is mentioned when it extends knowledge about friendship conflict.

Sibling relationships fit the definition of close relationships but have particular constraints associated with them (e.g., the relationship can only be terminated by death) that make them different from friendships. Therefore, we will limit our discussion of sibling relationships and focus on conflict between friends. The nature of conflict and friendship is discussed first, and current research in friendship conflict is discussed second.

✿ The Nature of Conflict and Friendship

As illustrated thus far in this book, conflict constitutes a wide variety of phenomena; the area of peer conflict presents no exception. For example, peer conflict has been operationalized as primarily negative phenomena, such as feelings of alienation and confrontation (Claes, 1992). Hartup (1992) noted that studies of children's conflict often focus on antagonistic behavior (e.g., Howes, 1983). Other scholars examine peer conflicts as composed of both constructive and destructive behaviors (e.g., Gottman, 1983; Sillars, 1980a, 1980b). In keeping with our goal to be representative of the literature, conflict in this chapter includes a variety of phenomena.

Often we will treat the conception of conflict between friends primarily as opposition, consistent with prior discussion. Maynard (1985) noted that opposition "is taken as the defining feature of children's disputes" (p. 211). However, examining conflict as opposition does not necessarily mean a focus on strings of disagreements or antagonisms only. As Gottman (1983) and Youniss (1980) illustrated, individuals have a variety of options when faced with a conflictual situation.

As previously noted, discussion of sibling conflict is limited in the current chapter. Shantz and Hobart (1989) succinctly reasoned that "because siblings are embedded within the family, their relationship is of particular, and probably unique, significance" (p. 76). In view of this central difference between siblings and friends, we stress friendship conflict. Sibling conflict is addressed in detail elsewhere (e.g., Katz, Kramer, & Gottman, 1992; Stillwell & Dunn, 1985).

Friendships are typically defined as closer than nonfriend peer relationships; however, the overall definition of friendship remains somewhat vague. Nonetheless, there are four central themes across definitions of friendships. First, as indicated previously, friendship is a voluntary association. Second, there are few social rules for enacting the relationship (Wiseman, 1986). Importantly, Blieszner and Adams (1992) cautioned that because there are *some* norms and expectations regarding friendship behaviors and formation, the relationship is not entirely voluntary. Third, several authors, in addition to those already mentioned, note the importance of equality and reciprocity in friendship (Hartup, 1992; Piaget, 1932; Smollar & Youniss, 1982; Youniss, 1980). Although friendships usually form between people with equal status, they sometimes entail status inequity (Rawlins, 1992; Youniss, 1980). Fourth, friendships are characterized by mutuality (Piaget, 1932; Rawlins, 1992). In summary, "At all ages, friendships reveal characteristics of mutuality and reciprocity which are founded on a voluntary interdependence" (Claes, 1992, p. 41).

Although people know the difference between friends and nonfriends from early childhood, their conception of what the relation entails and how to behave changes as people develop and mature (Berndt & Perry, 1986). For example, what is a common conflict interaction for young friends would be perceived as a cruel or com-

bative exchange among adults (Corsaro, 1981). Corsaro provided the
following example dialogue of 3-year-olds interacting:

> Denny (D), age 3.5, and Leah (L), age 3.2, are running and pretending
> to be lions. Joseph (J), age 3.2, watches from a distance. Glen (G), age
> 3.9, who had been playing with D earlier, approaches D and L. J follows
> closely behind G:
>
> **D-G:**   Grr-Grr. We don't like you.
> **L-G:**   Grr-Grr.
> **G-D:**   You were my friend a minute ago.
> **D-G:**   Yeah.
> **G-D:**   Well, if you keep going "grr," you can't be my friend anymore.
> **J-D:**   Yeah.
> **D-G:**   Well, then I'm not your friend.
> **L-GJ:** Yeah. Grr-Grr.
>
> L and D now run off toward climbing bars; G moves into sandpile with
> J and they begin digging. (p. 219)

Moreover, conflict appears to play a significant role in friendship
formation. One of our primary assumptions is that conflict is inevitable when people relate to one another. Youniss (1980) argued that
because friendships can last, even though "friends are individual
persons with interests and separate emotional lives to protect" (p. 208),
it is clear that friends' successful conflict management is a prereq-
uisite for lasting friendships.

Claes (1992) also found support for the significant role of conflict in
friendship. However, in this case, conflict was not necessarily good
for the relationship. Claes operationalized conflict emphasizing potential negative qualities of the phenomenon: [Conflict entailed] "feelings of alienation among friends and the presence of confrontations
and rivalry between friends" (p. 43). Not surprisingly, such conflict
was negatively related to overall adjustment and positively related to
psychopathology. In terms of importance, Claes (1992) reported that
the presence of this type of conflict (rather than number of friends and
close friends) predicted adjustment and psychopathology in adolescents. In other words, the presence of Claes's negative conflict, as
opposed to conflict defined as opposition or disagreement, is more
problematic for the adolescent than how many friends he or she has.

Claes (1992) concluded that conflictual relations of this negative type should be avoided. Still other research indicates that some types of conflict function to promote friendship formation for both children (e.g., Gottman, 1983) and adults (e.g., Hays, 1985).

In particular, children's conflicts with friends have been reported to benefit them in several ways. Katz et al. (1992) reviewed how conflict contributes to children's social development. For instance, Hay and Ross (1982) found that children refine their social skills through conflict. Rizzo (1989) argued that conflicts aid in the construction of friendships by underscoring children's specific expectations.

Given the centrality of development regarding both conflict and friendships, age differences provide a useful means for dividing the research findings on friends' conflicts. However, comparisons between age groups should be viewed as tentative estimates of the effect of development on friendship conflict. Hartup (1992) warned that methodological variation exists such that self-report methods are most common for adolescents and adults, whereas the findings for children are predominately based on observational methods. Accordingly, we attempt to isolate central themes for each age group. Although overlap between the age groups is inevitable, we found the following divisions useful: early childhood (2 years to 6 years), middle childhood (7 years to 11 years), adolescence (12 years to 18 years), and adults (18 years and up). These categories primarily represent distinctions made by researchers of peer conflict and friendships (e.g., Parker & Gottman, 1989).

ʒ♦ Conflict Between Early Childhood Friends (Age 2 to 6)

In early childhood, research themes include the nature of interaction and conflict, frequency and duration of conflict, and conflict issues.

The Nature of Interaction and Conflict

Several researchers have shown that children's friendships in early childhood emphasize playing and sharing (e.g., Youniss, 1980). Interaction in these friendships, then, focuses primarily on coordinating play for maximum enjoyment (Parker & Gottman, 1989). Youniss and Volpe (1978) found that when young children gave examples of interactions with friends, the children's descriptions were focused on a physical activity in which the interaction took place. The sample dialogue from Corsaro (1981) given previously also illustrates that conflicts about the friendship itself center on activities (i.e., playing lions).

Younger children manage conflict less successfully and less amicably than do older children (Gottman & Parkhurst, 1980; Renshaw & Asher, 1983). For example, Bakeman and Brownlee (1982) found that toddlers' conflicts ended only with adult intervention 20% of the time compared to preschoolers' 11%. In addition, toddlers' limited behavioral repertoire may indicate why they have less success in managing conflict. Hay and Ross (1982) found that in response to an antagonist, toddlers used forcible contact (16.5% of the time), gentle touch or offering of the object (23% of the time), and one-word statements such as "mine" or "no" (53% of the time). As children develop, they not only gain additional response options for conflict but also gradually obtain a broader understanding of the functional and promotive role of conflict in relationships (Selman, 1980).

Frequency and Duration of Conflict

Conflicts in early childhood are brief and rare (Shantz, 1987). Consistent with prior research, Hay and Ross (1982) found that the average duration of 21-month-old children's conflicts was 22.7 seconds and that they experienced an average of 2.3 conflicts per 15-minute period. In addition, the number of turns in these conflicts is usually limited to about five, further indicating that young children's conflicts reflect brief encounters (Eisenberg & Garvey, 1981; Hay & Ross, 1982; O'Keefe & Benoit, 1982).

Shantz (1987) warned that although such conflicts may be short and infrequent, they are nonetheless significant. She argued that "these events appear to have substantial affective meaning for the children involved" (p. 286). The affective meaning can be either positive or negative. Indeed, Parker and Gottman (1989) contended that younger children actually avoid conflict more than older children because of the ramifications that negative affect can have for the younger child's fantasy play; specifically, fantasy play requires complex coordination, which is threatened by conflict and negative emotions. Parker and

Gottman (1989) nonetheless noted that "if play is to be coordinated, it is simply not always possible to get one's own way" (p. 112). These authors concluded that conflicts with friends, however brief or rare, play an important role in children's development of social skills.

Conflict Issues

Research in early childhood conflict behavior has consistently revealed that the most common conflict issue for toddlers and preschoolers centers on object possession (e.g., Berndt, 1982; Shantz, 1987). In a review of more than 20 studies, Hay (1984) found that, on the average, 71% of young children's conflicts involved struggles over objects. Hay and Ross (1982) reported that "the overwhelming majority [of the conflicts] were in whole or in part struggles for objects" (p. 108). Garvey (1984), cited in Shantz (1987), illustrated a typical object-centered conflict between two preschoolers:

A: That's mine. (Approaches partner B who has started to play with truck)
B: This is not. No. (Moves truck)
A: It's mine. (Stands, looking down at partner and truck)
B: Well, I'm using it. I'm using it.
A: Could I take it home?
B: No, it's the school's.
A: Yes, I am take it home.
B: You don't have a house, you live here.
A: No, I live at home, Lake Charles Avenue.
B: Well, I'm using that. I'm using it.
A: Could I take that home?
B: Yes, okay. (But doesn't relinquish the truck)
A: Could I take that home? (Speaks more softly than before)
B: Okay, but, but, but I'm using it. (Turns away from A). I'll give it to you when you're gonna go. (Continues to play with truck. A moves away from B). (p. 302)

Although such object-centered conflicts appear less common as toddlers grow older, object conflicts are still frequent among preschool children.

Hay (1984) noted that some researchers argued that conflicts involving objects were not truly social conflicts because they were "impersonally motivated." Hay (1984) contended that "the notion that struggles for the possession of objects are 'socially blind' does not fully take into account the social significance as well as the objective properties of those objects" (p. 16). For example, very young children make ownership claims to objects (Bakeman & Brownlee, 1982; Eckerman, Whatley, & Kutz, 1975). Bakeman and Brownlee (1982) found that the object conflicts of toddlers and preschoolers may be rule governed in that even young children appear to operate under the "prior possession" rule (i.e., the first to possess the object shall enjoy ownership rights). In addition, Eckerman, Whatley, and McGehee (1979) observed that 1-year-olds showed more interest in a toy if another child had the toy. Of course, the desire to own material objects extends into adulthood. Both Bakeman and Brownlee (1982) and Hay (1984) noted that conflicts over possessions and resources continue throughout life. Clearly, object conflicts function as social conflicts at least in rudimentary ways (e.g., Hay & Ross, 1982): They are the building blocks and content for battle.

Other conflict issues for young children include those over personal space, or social intrusiveness (Hay, 1984). As children get older, intrusiveness conflicts become centered less on the physical environment (i.e., objects and space) and more on the actions or interference of others on one's goals (Hay, 1984; Shantz, 1987). Conflicts also begin to involve violations of social norms. For example, Fagot (1977) found that children view violations of gender roles in play negatively. Based on the research into conflict issues of young children, Shantz (1987) drew the following conclusions: First, almost any behavior can serve as the impetus for a conflict; second, conflicts may appear to be over one issue but actually may center on something else; and third, the initial focus of a conflict may not be the focus of the entire conflict.

✿ Conflict Between Middle Childhood Friends (Age 7 to 11)

Children's social worlds change greatly in elementary school through opportunities to interact with many more people. Their peer group becomes more complex (Parker & Gottman, 1989). Several researchers (e.g., Hartup, 1992; Parker & Gottman, 1989) have noted that because of such changes in a child's social world, as well as developmental changes, middle childhood is when friendship becomes a "relation proper" (Youniss, 1980). In addition to friendships becoming more meaningful, conflict in these relationships also becomes more salient. For example, Shantz (1993) found that 7-year-olds not only remember conflicts with close others versus nonclose others, but these children also report "learning a lesson" from their conflicts. The central themes in the research on conflict in middle childhood focus on the nature of interaction and conflict, conflict and friendship formation, and the frequency and issues of conflict.

The Nature of Interaction and Conflict

Reciprocity represents one characteristic of interaction and conflict that becomes more apparent during middle childhood as compared to early childhood (Berndt, 1979). Friendship researchers consistently note the importance of relational reciprocity for both children and adults (e.g., Claes, 1992; Levitt, Weber, Clark, & McDonnell, 1985). MacCombie (1978) illustrated the frequency of reciprocal verbal and nonverbal behaviors as well as expressions of emotion in reporting median correlations between the specific behaviors of two interacting children as .7 for 2- to 5-year-olds and .9 for 6- to 9-year-olds. This finding indicates a substantial reciprocity effect for both groups, and it is greater for slightly older children.

In terms of conflict behavior specifically, reciprocation represents the most common strategy in middle childhood (Youniss, 1980). Youniss (1980) found negative chaining, or continued reciprocation of negative behaviors, more frequent in middle childhood than it is in early adolescence. However, such conflicts were equally likely to end either in a positive or negative outcome. Youniss (1980) provided one 8-year-old's description of a nonresolved conflict that is clearly reciprocal:

> Like if they were best friends and I asked if I could play . . . and she says no. / Then I would say, "I hate you. I won't be your friend anymore." / She wouldn't talk to me. / I wouldn't talk to her. (p. 142)

Hartup and Laursen (1993) noted that if children in such reciprocal interactions avoided aggressive behaviors yet maintained their level of insistence, the conflict would likely end in compromise.

Youniss (1980) observed that some children had a more sophisticated understanding of reciprocity. Such children appeared to understand that although they were entitled to reciprocate their friends'
negative behavior, nonreciprocation or nonretaliation might be more
effective. For example, Youniss quotes one 10-year-old:

> He steals their things. / Don't play with the person who stole it. / He'd
> give it back and say he was sorry. / He'd play with them again. (p. 212)

Youniss (1980) contended that, in such cases, the offended child
realizes that "friendship cannot be maintained with purely negative
exchanges" (p. 217). Moreover, the child does not ignore the offense
but, instead, unilaterally initiates a positive behavior in hope that the
offending party will then reciprocate positively and apologize or
repair the offense in some way. Similarly, Gottman (1983) found that
"weak demands" (i.e., those demands that help the other child save
face because the initiator hedges or allows the other to refuse) were
likely to be more successful, and such demands were more common
between children who subsequently became friends than between
children who did not form a friendship.

Conflict and Friendship Formation

Insider and outsider views on children's conflicts differ regarding
the importance of conflict in friendship formation (Hartup, 1992). In
other words, from the *child's* perspective, disagreements (Smollar &
Youniss, 1982) and frequency of conflict (Shantz, 1987) constitute the
main reasons why friendships are not formed. On the other hand,
Gottman's (1983) observations revealed that neither frequency of
disagreements nor the ratio of agreements to disagreements predicts
friendship formation. Instead, he found that friends, versus nonfriends, engaged in more of *both* agreements and disagreements.
Conflict behavior predicted friendship formation in combination
with other variables, including successful information exchange and
clear, connected communication behaviors. The latter category con-
sisted of messages that clarified a previous message or sought
clarification of another's message *and* illustrated that children were
responding to each other such that their messages were connected.
Moreover, conflict management processes, rather than number of

disagreements, were also more influential in friendship formation. In addition, Hartup (1989) concluded that, based on studies of children's aggression and conflict, conflict management is central to determining both social acceptance and rejection.

Hartup (1992) drew two conclusions based on recent findings. First, conflict functions both constructively and destructively in friendship formation. Second, a dialectic between agreement and disagreement must be managed in order to establish the common ground that is a basis for friendships (e.g., Doyle, 1982). It appears that the reason children cite disagreements as barriers to friendships is that they primarily recall those managed through destructive means. This explanation also finds support from the observation that although *de*structive conflict may be a major deterrent to friendship (e.g., Gottman, 1983), *con*structive conflict appears to be essential to friendship formation (e.g., Burleson & Samter, 1994; Parker & Gottman, 1989).

Frequency and Issues of Conflict

Based on the research, Hartup (1989) drew the conclusion that "children's friendships encompass a considerable amount of conflict" (p. 65). Although conflict comprises a central feature of middle childhood relationships, variations and implications of frequency provide further clarification of the phenomenon. For example, although Gottman (1983) found that the occurrence of agreements more than disagreements predicts friendship formation, Shantz (1986) observed that higher rates of conflict also predicted whether a peer was liked or disliked (two separate measures). Interestingly, Shantz found that a peer who engaged in frequent conflicts was more often disliked than peers who engaged in aggressive behavior within isolated conflicts. Importantly, Shantz (1986) found no relationship between being liked and frequency of conflict *or* use of aggressive behaviors.

Furman (1987) found similar results in a self-report study of 8-year-olds at camp. The author compared children's ratings of both acquaintances made at camp and peers they previously knew. The conflict among previously acquainted children was stable over the period of one week, as was conflict with peers who were rated high on a friendliness measure. However, conflict was significantly *more* frequent both as peers became acquainted over the week and for peers rated low and medium in terms of friendliness. Furman's findings illustrate that, similar to friendship formation, children's process of acquaintanceship entails substantial amounts of conflict. In addition, the finding that conflict rates stabilize in established relationships is also interesting.

Further research might explore the extent of stability of conflict rates, as well as how conflict stability continues as participants age throughout childhood and in later life. For example, Berndt and Perry (1986) reported that younger (7- to 11-year-olds) participants reported fewer conflicts with friends versus acquaintances, whereas older participants (13-year-olds) reported that conflict rates were about the same for both. Such changes may be due to developmental factors or alternative perceptions affecting views regarding both relationships and conflicts.

Research into the issues of conflict also aids in understanding children's conflicts. For example, Shantz (1993) found the conflict topics most salient to 7-year-olds were person control issues, including teasing, name calling, and psychological harm (20%); physical harm (20%); social and friendship rules (16%); and facts and opinions (10%). Conflicts over possession of objects were also recalled. These conflicts were between close others, which included both friends and enemies. Shantz's findings provide some evidence for the inconsistencies that arise between insider and outsider perspectives on children's conflicts. Perhaps what children conceptualize, reference, and remember as conflict behavior varies substantively and categorically from adult/researcher perspectives. Although some research attempts to isolate children's perceptions of conflict (e.g., Youniss, 1980), more consideration of how to reconcile insider and outsider perspectives appears warranted (Hartup, 1992).

❧ Conflict Between Adolescent Friends (Age 12 to 18)

Just as relations with friends change greatly from early to middle childhood, they develop further as children move into adolescence. Significant changes in conflict management also occur with these more general relational changes (Hartup, 1992). La Gaipa and Wood (1981) asserted that two changes in particular differentiate the adolescent from other children: "The adolescent has to solve problems of

ego identity and autonomy; there is a shift from childhood depend-
ence to adult independence" (p. 170). In order to accomplish the
desired autonomy, the adolescent pulls away from parents and family,
both emotionally and communicatively, and intensifies peer relationships so that "peers become both allies in the effort to deal with the
challenges of independence and themselves potential sources of grati-
fication" (Weiss, 1986, p. 104).

Moreover, Claes (1992) commented that adolescent friendships
were vital for social development as well as for psychological development and adjustment. Parker and Gottman (1989) contended that the
functions of friendship at this age were to facilitate self-exploration
and the integration of logic and emotions. These authors further
asserted that these functions were served through a new emphasis on
intimate self-disclosure.

Several researchers have deduced that adolescent friendships, as
opposed to younger children's friendships, entail more intimacy and
value it more (e.g., Berndt & Perry, 1986; Selman, 1981; Sharabany,
Gershoni, & Hofman, 1981). For example, as adolescents age, they
increasingly differentiate between intimate and nonintimate friends
and reduce their number of intimate friends. Such changes affect the
interaction behavior of adolescents. The nature of conflict and conflict
issues reflects these developmental changes.

The Nature of Conflict

Although increased intimacy characterizes relationships with friends,
adolescent conflict tends to be both less intense with friends as compared to siblings, parents, and other peer relationships (Laursen, 1993)
and less negative (Claes, 1992). Parker and Gottman (1989) observed
the following dialogue between two friends when one was disclosing
a dissatisfaction:

Jane: I feel kind of icky about the past two weeks.
Suzie: What? What in the past two weeks do you feel icky about?
Jane: It was like "Hi, Jane," "Hi, Suzie," [*giggle*] you know, [*giggle*].
Suzie: Yeah.
Jane: "Hi, Jane," "Hi, Suzie."
Suzie: We didn't communicate. I haven't been communicating much
with anybody.

Jane: I understand that. But I felt like, you know, Janet was . . .

Suzie: Janet had taken your place?

Jane: Yeah. That's what I felt like.

Suzie: Janet's not gonna take your place, kiddo, [*sigh*]. How many times do I have to tell you that?

Jane: I'm insecure, you know. (p. 122)

A younger child in a similar situation would probably display more negative affect. But the adolescent has matured to a level at which he or she not only recognizes that the other person may have legitimate reasons for behavior but also desires to understand the friend's motivations (Berndt & Perry, 1986).

Such a shift toward sophisticated thoughts regarding conflict accompanies the shift from perceiving others as merely actors to perceiving them as people (Hartup, 1992; Selman, 1980; Shantz, 1987). Shantz (1987) summarized studies suggesting that as children age, they become oriented toward the future and toward developing friendships during conflict, whereas younger children focus on the immediate right or concrete possession that constitutes the object of conflict. Berndt and Perry (1986) found that adolescents understood they could both support a friend and engage in conflict with that friend (see also Selman, 1980). Younger children, on the other hand, assumed that conflict and support were incompatible (Berndt & Perry, 1986). In addition, Hartup and Laursen (1993) reported that adolescents differentiated between minor conflicts (e.g., behavioral annoyances) and major conflicts (e.g., violations of trust).

Conflict Issues

As is true of other age groups, the issues of adolescents' conflicts reflect their development. Significant changes in the adolescent's social world affect his or her interaction behavior (Parker & Gottman, 1989). Hartup (1992) reported that conflicts over objects are largely nonexistent for adolescents. In addition, disagreements no longer satisfactorily explain why friendship formation does not ensue; instead, conflicts of *personality* block friendship formation (Smollar & Youniss, 1982). Laursen (1993) related that conflicts with friends specifically "concerned interpersonal standards of friendship and heterosexual behavior" (p. 546). Additional conflict issues for this age group include ideas and opinions, teasing/criticism, and annoying behaviors (Laursen, 1989).

⚜ Conflict Between Adult Friends (Age 18 and Older)

Conflict in adult friendships has not been examined as extensively as children's friendship conflicts. Blieszner and Adams (1992) observed that behavioral processes, including conflict, have not been comprehensively and systematically analyzed in adult friendships. Of the "scattered" existing studies, interaction research focuses on self-disclosure and social support, with few studies specifically addressing conflict and friendship (Blieszner & Adams, 1992). Moreover, most of the research involves college students. Some studies focus on older adults, whereas middle-aged adults are the least studied. In the following discussion, some possible reasons for the meager amount of research on the topic are examined. In addition, the role of conflict in adult friendship is discussed, as well as the strategies and issues of conflict in these relationships. Finally, some new directions for research in adult friendship conflict are explored.

Explaining Insufficient Research
in Adult Friendship Conflict

One reason for the dearth of research on adult friendship conflicts may reflect an ideology that romance and family are supposedly more important than are friends in adulthood. Some scholars comment that friendships are no longer a priority for adults. For example, Weiss (1986) contended that in early adulthood (22 to 23 years), people begin focusing their relational efforts on establishing a new attachment bond. In other words, individuals focus on finding and beginning a relationship with a life partner or spouse (see also Fiebert & Wright, 1989). Because of the new focus on attachment over affiliative bonds, as well as career moves, friendships are likely to fade away (Matthews, 1986; Weiss, 1986). The primacy and social importance of attachment bonds in particular are underscored by the larger social system. For example, Braiker and Kelley (1979) cited this primacy as their first reason for focusing their studies of conflict in close relationships on marital and premarital dyads. These authors asserted that "it goes without saying that the course of premarital and marriage dyads is highly important in societies like ours, which rely on the family for such functions as moral training and the instilling of work motivation" (p. 135).

However, friendships also serve important functions in adulthood. Rawlins (1992) argued that because young adults focus on finding a partner and beginning their careers, friends are essential in that they help each other make such important decisions. However, he continued that, "ironically, the praxic functions of friendship at this stage involve helping each other make decisions regarding self, marriage, and career, which ultimately constrict the opportunities for involvement with friends" (p. 123). Rawlins noted that because of time constraints, individuals must discriminate among potential friends as well as among established friends. During young adulthood, the processes of discrimination among and negotiations with friends help to shape a person's self-defining values. Rawlins argued that even though people may reduce both their numbers of friends and time spent with friends, the friendship relationship remained important.

Another explanation for the dearth of research into adult friendship conflict holds that conflict is simply not salient to adult friends. Rawlins (1994) observed that time and distance often separate adult friends. In such cases, he asserted that conflict represents "an issue of the past" and no longer emerges as a part of present interactions between adult friends. Matthews (1986) interviewed older adults regarding their friendships across their life span. Although one entire chapter was devoted to maintaining and terminating friendships, conflict and conflict management were never mentioned. In this case, the exclusion of conflict issues may derive from the research methods: Because participants gave their biographies in terms of their friendships, perhaps conflict was not a salient issue to them in terms of either maintaining or terminating their relationships. Therefore, it appears that interviewing adults may not yield extensive data on conflict management. Perhaps observations of adult friends would provide a very different picture of conflict in their relationships.

The Role of Conflict in Adult Friendships

Some existing research on the topic illustrates that conflict is indeed integral to adults' relations with friends. From an exchange perspective, Hays (1985) noted that friendships cost individuals emotional aggravation but that people may consider this cost negligible in view of the benefits derived from their friendships. As in the case of children, conflict plays a central role in friendship formation and maintenance. Hays (1985) summarized that "these findings suggest that interpersonal dissatisfactions or costs are inescapable aspects of personal relationships and so, to some degree, may become immaterial" (p. 922). Moreover, working through conflict issues and differences, dyads may come to regard their relationships as unique and hence value them more (Braiker & Kelley, 1979; Hays, 1985). Hays (1985) advocated the need for additional research into the specifics of how conflicts function in friendships.

Dykstra (1990) similarly found that conflict was part of friendship interactions. Thirty-eight percent of her sample of older adults reported that they argued with close network members (network included partners, kin, and friends). Counter to expectations, conflict was not less frequent in friendships as opposed to other relational types. Instead, Dykstra found that a combination of two variables (i.e., enjoyment and conflict) best illustrated the difference between friendships and other relationships. Conflict existed in all relationship types. However, in friendship, the levels of enjoyment were higher than the level of conflict, whereas in other relationships the reverse was often true. Moreover, she found that similar to research into children's relationships, voluntary relationships (e.g., friendships) obtained the highest levels of enjoyment relative to reported conflict (i.e., friends reported more enjoyment than conflict). Friends had the highest enjoyment/conflict ratio, significantly higher than that enjoyed by romantic partners and siblings. The findings of Dykstra (1990) and Hays (1985) indicate that conflict does surface in adult friendships in benign forms. Their research also indicates a need for more specific information on adult conflict interaction behaviors.

Conflict Strategies and Issues

Healey and Bell (1990) examined the strategic responses of individuals when offended by an adult friend. Conflict in this study was operationalized as an event in which a friend said or did something that caused the individual to become dissatisfied with the relationship. As such, the conflicts were serious because of their adverse effect on the relationship. The authors investigated connections between the individual's friendship network and the individual's response to the offense in terms of Rusbult's (1987) exit-voice-loyalty-neglect model (see Chapter 5). Healey and Bell found that conflict of this nature was primarily a dyadic event, and network factors did not predict strategy use. Instead, seriousness of the conflict strongly predicted the destructive responses of exit (e.g., threatening to leave the friend, leaving the friend) and neglect (e.g., embarrassing the friend, ignoring the friend).

Friendships are fragile. And in cases of serious conflict between friends, either exit or neglect may be likely because of the potential "mortality" of the relationship (Rawlins, 1994). Rawlins (1994) explained how friendships are mortal insofar as "Friendship lacks the legal and/or religious sanctions buttressing marriages, the economic contracts reinforcing partnerships and business associations, and the blood ties linking kin throughout their lives" (p. 277). Perhaps more than in other relationships, one can appropriately manage relational problems by simply walking away from an adult friend. For example, Baxter (1979) found that in ending relationships, friends prefer to avoid direct confrontation and discussion of the issue.

To understand the seriousness of conflict issues, Argyle and Furnham (1983) investigated sources of close relationship conflict of both young adults and middle-aged adults. Participants rated friends, siblings, parents, children, work colleagues, and work associates on both satisfaction and conflict. The authors found that people reported high satisfaction for friends, particularly same-sex friends, and that conflict frequency for friends was relatively low. Moreover, friends' conflicts centered on issues such as competition for jobs or promotions, competition for the affections of others, and having different beliefs or values. Opposite-sex friends competed less for jobs but conflicted more in terms of discussing personal problems and understanding each other. And conflict in the form of criticism was much less common for friends than it was for either spouses or kin. Finally, Argyle and Furnham reported some age differences with regard to conflict. First, older people experienced less conflict in long-standing relationships, whereas younger adults experienced more conflict across all their relationships.

Age of adults may affect conflict issues as well as conflict frequency and amount. For example, Fisher, Reid, and Melendez (1989) found that one source of conflict for older adult friends involved whether or not the friend adhered to role expectations given his or her age. For comparative illustration, the role expectations of importance to children are focused on gender stereotypes (e.g., Fagot, 1977). Of course, the issue is that research on conflict over role expectations for all the ages in between is lacking. The evolution of interpersonal conflict over the life span warrants further scholarly attention.

New Directions for Research in Adult Friendship Conflict

This chapter focused primarily on friendship. However, adult friendships may not be as easily distinguishable from other close relationship types as are children's. Adults' friends are frequently their coworkers, roommates, or relatives. The blending of relationship types may have implications for the friendship. For example, when adult friends are also work colleagues and the job changes or ends, the relationship is very often directly affected (Matthews, 1986). Furthermore, college roommate relationships resemble both friendships (e.g., nonkin, interdependent) and sibling relationships (e.g., shared living space). Sillars (1980a) found differences in roommates based on relational satisfaction. Also, conflict management for the roommates is likely influenced by the conditions under which the relationship was initiated and maintained (Berscheid & Graziano, 1979). These brief examples indicate that conflict in such relationships may surface differently than it does in "pure" friendships. The influence of these relationship type constraints on friends' conflict behaviors merits further investigation.

As previously mentioned, conclusions based on comparisons across studies and across ages are tentative. Another thorny area for comparison concerns research on sex differences. For example, Argyle and Furnham's (1983) findings regarding opposite-sex friends do not parallel other research (e.g., Buhrke & Fuqua, 1987; Metts & Cupach, 1993; Rose, 1985). The latter studies primarily focused on opposite-sex friendships of young adults, whereas Argyle and Furnham (1983) examined relationships of both young and middle-aged adults. Inconsistencies may arise from methodological differences or may be due to the age of the participants. Rawlins (1992) noted that as children develop, their preferences for opposite- versus same-sex friends change so that younger children appear to have no preference, school-aged children apparently prefer same-sex friends, and adolescents appear to value both same- and opposite-sex friends. Perhaps adult preferences also cycle through change, which specifically suggests three issues: (a) Future research needs to examine conflict between opposite-sex friends more specifically; (b) future research needs to compare conflict between same- and opposite-sex friends with regard to issues, frequency, and management; and (c) such research needs to extend over the life span.

An understanding of conflict over the life span may extend knowledge regarding the developmental process itself. For example, beginning in early childhood, people learn that retaliation or reciprocation of negativity is not an effective method of conflict management. Youniss (1980) discovered that children and adolescents learn to use nonconfrontation or avoidance strategically when a friend commits an offense. Children noted that, most often, the offender would reciprocate the positivity of the avoider and apologize or make amends in some way.

In addition, adults appear to be aware of the principle of reciprocity in friendships and interact strategically because of it. For example, Matthews's (1986) sample of older adults reported how friendships ended; however, none of the participants described the end as a result of a major confrontation. Apparently, adults prefer to avoid the negative fallout that may result from reciprocal interactions in conflicts. Similarly, Sillars (1980b) explored reciprocation of conflict behaviors between college roommates, relying on attribution theory. He found that roommates who attributed the cause of conflict to the other person were very likely to reciprocate—and thereby escalate—negative, distributive messages. However, roommates who attributed the cause of conflict internally to themselves were more likely to reciprocate cooperative, integrative actions. Similar to reciprocation, other specific conflict issues and behavior vary across the life span.

Unfortunately, developmental approaches focus predominantly on children rather than on adult friendships. Of course, people continue to develop and adapt upon leaving adolescence and college. The limited research that compares adult friendships of different ages indicates that people do change from early to middle to later adulthood (e.g., Blieszner & Adams, 1992). Research and theory need to explore the ways in which such development affects conflict interaction behavior.

Rawlins's (1994) dialectical approach to friendships may further illustrate how nonconfrontation or avoidance specifically functions in relationships. For example, Rawlins observed that people strive to maintain balance between sets of two simultaneous pulls in opposite directions, such as the freedom to be independent and the freedom to be dependent. Failure to maintain balance between the poles is likely to end in conflict (intrapersonal, interpersonal, or both). Hence, it appears that if people work at maintaining balance, they in effect may prevent conflict (cf. Baxter, 1994).

Perhaps another reason why conflict does not readily appear salient to adults rests on the assumption that conflict first and foremost entails oppositions. An alternative approach to the study of conflict in friendship would examine interactive processes that function to prevent conflict or oppositions from occurring.

Nonetheless, conflict between adult friends requires further investigation. Given the importance of conflict to parent-child relationships, children's friendships, and romantic relationships, and given the research cited here, conflict probably plays a critical role in adult friendships. The few studies that directly address conflict demonstrate how conflict is relevant to people in friendships beyond adolescence. If, as we argue in Chapter 1, conflict occurs as an inescapable activity of close relationships, conflict should be salient in adult friendships as it is in other relationships.

⋅ₐ Conclusions

Research on conflict between friends provides several ideas for contemplation. Three specific conclusions can be drawn. First, and consistent with our third assumption in Chapter 1, friendships particularly differ from other relationships in terms of how partners manage conflict. For example, at all ages there appears to be a tendency for friends to manage conflict more amicably and less aggressively than conflicts with siblings, parents, or romantic partners.

Second, conflict management with friends appears to change over the life span. Even though cross-age group comparisons of different studies must be made tentatively, differences between groups are nonetheless discernible. The topics, nature of interaction, and frequency of conflict differ in early childhood, middle childhood, and adolescence. In addition, these same areas are also different from childhood to adulthood.

For example, toddlers' repertoire of behavioral responses to conflict is limited to using forcible contact, giving in, or using one-word statements such as "no" (Hay & Ross, 1982). As children get older, they gradually gain sophistication in their management of conflict with friends by using face-saving "weak demands" and positivity. By the time a person reaches adolescence, he or she realizes that the friend has reasons for behaving. The adolescent manages conflict with a greater sensitivity to the other person's motivation. Finally, adults appear to avoid conflict in friendships more than younger people do. Clearly, changes occur in conflict management across the life span.

Third, conflict seems to be an integral part of the initiation and maintenance of friendships. Particularly the research on friendship formation indicates that conflict is not only inescapable but that it plays an important role in determining who people choose as friends. For example, Gottman (1983) found that when children managed conflict constructively, they were more likely to establish a friendship. In addition, Hartup (1992) surmised that conflict management was central to determining both social acceptance and rejection.

Moreover, other research illustrated how conflict influences the maintenance of friendships. Furman (1987) found that children had fewer conflicts once a relationship was established with a friend. In addition, children often cite frequent conflict as a reason for terminating a friendship. In the case of adults, friendships are apparently maintained by avoiding conflict or by finding ways to prevent conflict interactions. In short, conflict plays a pivotal role in friendships as it does in other close relationships.

Although a great deal of research exists in the area of conflict between friends, many questions remain. Several important gaps in the literature have been identified. For example, the link between conflict and development requires further investigation. In particular, more research programs examining conflict across age groups and over time are needed. Additional research is also needed to explore conflict in adult friendships.

5

Conflict in Dating and Marital Relationships

W e now turn to the rather broad domain of conflict in "romantic" relationships. In particular, we highlight some key findings contained in the copious literature on conflict among dating couples and in marital relationships. Our review pertains to relationships that exhibit various degrees of interdependence and relational commitment and tend to be marked by physical as well as psychological intimacy. As in the previous chapters, our review is selective and representative rather than comprehensive. We first briefly review evidence regarding the occurrence and developmental course of conflict, as well as issues that precipitate conflict. Next, we summarize key findings regarding the relationship between conflict management behaviors and relational quality. Finally, we identify some relational and perceptual factors that qualify and constrain conflict management processes and outcomes.

❧ The Nature of Conflict in Dating and Marital Relationships

The Frequency of Conflict

Accurate data about the frequency of conflict in relationships elude us—particularly given the diverse conceptions among researchers (and relational partners) regarding what constitutes conflict. Still, studies do suggest a range of conflict frequency. Using a semistructured diary method, Lloyd (1987) had 25 premarital dating couples record conflict interactions over a 14-day period. Couples reported an average of 4.6 disagreements for the 2-week period. Moreover, male and female partners largely agreed on the number of conflicts reported, $r = .81$. McGonagle, Kessler, and Schilling (1992) surveyed a demographically diverse community sample of married couples about the frequency of disagreements in their relationships. Interviews were conducted at two different points in time, 3 years apart. The vast majority of participants reported an average of one or two "unpleasant disagreements" per month. The accuracy of these retrospective estimates was verified using a random subsample of respondents who kept daily diaries. Interestingly, the vast majority of respondents (90%) reported no or relatively little change in disagreement frequency over a 3-year period. Vincent et al. (1975) reported a study wherein distressed couples engaged in approximately one conflict a day on the average (i.e., $M = 5.4$ conflicts over a 5-day period). But nondistressed couples experienced only one conflict every 5 days (i.e., $M = 1.0$ conflict over a 5-day period). These data suggest that conflict frequencies can vary dramatically depending on the satisfaction level of participants.

The Developmental Course of Conflict in Relationships

Despite the voluminous research on interpersonal conflict, little attention has been devoted to understanding the dynamics of how conflict functions over the temporal course of a relationship (Gottman & Levenson, 1992). Fundamentally, researchers concentrate on how conflict varies across developmental stages of relationships and how conflict at particular stages may associate with subsequent conflict, relational stability, and satisfaction.

In their original investigation, Braiker and Kelley (1979) interviewed 22 married couples who answered questions about four stages in their relationship history: casual dating, serious dating, engagement, and the first 6 months of marriage. The researchers found that conflict-negativity (i.e., frequency of reports of conflict and negative feelings; see Chapter 2) significantly increased when moving from casual to serious dating. Thereafter, conflict levels remained stable (neither increasing nor decreasing) through the stages of engagement and marriage.

Similarly, Lloyd and Cate (1985) conducted retrospective interviews with 97 individuals who reported on a serious premarital relationship that had terminated. Their findings indicated that as commitment and interdependence in the relationship increased, so did levels of conflict. Conflict increased markedly when commitment first declined and then leveled off until the end of the relationship. In a study of 107 divorced individuals, Ponzetti and Cate (1987) explored changes in conflict across stages of the marital dissolution process. They found that conflict increased from initial recognition of divorce to discussion and then decreased once action was formally initiated to secure a legal dissolution.

Given the limitations of retrospective interviews, longitudinal studies are necessary to verify developmental changes in conflict. Kelly, Huston, and Cate (1985) also employed retrospective interviews with newly married couples reflecting back on three stages of their courtship. Two years later, couples were contacted, and they completed the conflict and other relational measures, including marital satisfaction and adjustment. Results indicated that levels of premarital conflict predicted later levels of marital conflict. Moreover, higher levels of premarital conflict were negatively associated with marital satisfaction, primarily for women. The authors suggested that the effects of continuing conflict in a relationship can accumulate and erode affective ties in the long run, despite the fact that conflict and affection are independent during courtship.

Berg and McQuinn (1986) studied 38 dating couples early in the formation of their relationships and again 4 months later. Using the Braiker and Kelley (1979) conflict scale, the authors found that conflict did not change over time nor did it distinguish between continuing and lapsed relationships. Consistent with this finding, Felmlee, Sprecher, and Bassin (1990) found that conflict levels did not accelerate the rate of breakup for premarital relationships.

Sprecher and Felmlee (1993) compared individuals in three types of premarital relationships over 3 months: those whose relationships destabilized or dissolved, those whose relationships remained stable, and those whose relationships increased in commitment. Conflict increased over time for the dissolving relationships but remained constant in the stable and growing relationships. Moreover, higher levels of love predicted higher levels of conflict later on. The authors summarized the implications of these and other findings by noting that conflict in a premarital relationship is not necessarily good or bad. It may simply "be a reflection of the degree of involvement and interdependence of a couple in partnership that is becoming more serious over time" (Sprecher & Felmlee, 1993, p. 11). More important than the mere presence or frequency of conflict are the dynamics regarding the content and management of conflict.

Conflict Topics and Issues

The potential "topics" of conflict that concern relational partners are virtually infinite. Issues related to communication, sex, jealousy, housework, finances, and the like emerge most frequently in studies of marital conflict and divorce (e.g., Gottman, 1979, 1994; Mead, Vatcher, Wyne, & Roberts, 1990). In an effort to capture at a global level types of issues or events that create conflict, a number of scholars have offered categorical schemes. Kelley and colleagues (see Braiker & Kelley, 1979) discovered three hierarchically organized levels of conflict problems that correspond to the various levels of interdependence that couples exhibit. In increasing levels of generality, these conflicts regard the following:

1. Specific and concrete behaviors (e.g., he leaves the cap off of the shampoo bottle; she interrupts conversation)
2. Relational rules and norms (e.g., he doesn't call if he is running late; she doesn't show him respect)
3. Personality traits (e.g., he's a slob; she's an alcoholic)

In addition, Kelley et al. (1978) identified a fourth type of conflict that potentially cuts across the other three types—conflict about the process of conflict itself. This includes complaints about communication behaviors such as nagging, withdrawing, sulking, temper tantrums, and so forth.

Peterson (1983) examined detailed accounts of conflict interactions and discerned four conditions that most frequently precipitate episodes of conflict. These include criticism, illegitimate demand, rebuff, and cumulative annoyance. In addition to these categories, Witteman (1992) observed the occurrence of noncumulative annoyance (i.e., a recognized difference in attitude, lifestyle, or opinion that has not occurred often) and mutual cumulative annoyance (in which both relational partners are involved, such as one partner displaying insufficient attention or affection to the other).

Research on conversational complaint episodes also sheds light on sources of conflict in intimate relationships (Alberts, 1988, 1989, 1990). Complaints that are made not only *to* a partner but also *about* a partner are particularly face threatening (Cupach & Metts, 1994). Such complaints commonly create defensiveness and can escalate into open conflict (Alberts & Driscoll, 1992).

Alberts (1989) interviewed couples in an effort to characterize the content of different kinds of complaints. She identified five primary complaint types:

1. Behavioral (e.g., "Why haven't I had a cooked meal all week?")
2. Personal characteristics (e.g., "You're a snob.")
3. Performance (e.g., "You're driving too fast.")
4. Complaining (e.g., "You're always complaining.")
5. Personal appearance (e.g., "You have a fat butt and better lose weight.")

In an analysis of couples' interactions during complaint episodes, Alberts (1988) found that maladjusted (e.g., dissatisfied) couples were more likely to engage in and reciprocate personal characteristic complaints than were adjusted couples. Certainly such complaints are among the most face threatening and are most likely to result in interpersonal conflict.

As indicated in Chapter 1, *conflict* refers to discrete, isolated disagreements as well as chronic relational problems. One important source of serious conflict derives from the literature on relational rule violations. Metts (1994) found that the most frequently listed relational transgressions included: having sexual intercourse outside of the primary relationship, wanting to date others, and deceiving the partner. Other transgressions mentioned by more than 5% of respondents included: violating a confidence; violating privacy of the relationship; forgetting plans and special occasions; failing to reciprocate sentiments of love, affection, or commitment; being jealous or untrusting; breaking an important promise; changing important plans; being physically abusive; not being there in a time of need; and not fighting fairly. Similarly, Jones and Burdette (1994) discovered types of betrayal in interpersonal relationships, the majority of which "concerned violations of trust, commitment, and generalized relationship expectations" (p. 255). These incidents of betrayal, listed in order of the frequency of occurrence, included the following:

1. Extramarital affairs
2. Lies
3. Betrayed confidence
4. Two-timing
5. Jilting
6. Lack of support
7. Ignoring/avoiding
8. Criticism
9. Gossip

❧ Dimensions of Conflict Behavior

One reason the literature on conflict management in dating and marital relationships occupies so much journal space is that researchers study conflict "behavior" at several levels of abstraction. As we indicated in Chapters 1 and 2, investigators examine a range of behaviors, from relatively microscopic verbal behaviors and sequences to more global styles and strategies for handling conflict. And whereas some researchers investigate particular episodes of conflict, others obtain information about conflict tendencies in the relationship generally. Regardless of the level of generality, three common dimensions are used to characterize conflict management behaviors.

Perhaps the most fundamental feature of conflict management concerns the dimension of engagement versus avoidance (e.g., Hocker & Wilmot, 1991; Raush, Barry, Hertel, & Swain, 1974; Sillars & Wilmot, 1994). Conflict engagement implies overt verbal confrontation of conflict issues, whereas avoidance suggests withdrawal and aversion to dealing directly with conflict issues. There are obviously degrees of directness/indirectness, activity/passivity, unequivocality/ equivocality that characterize the various behaviors exhibited in conflict situations (Sternberg & Dobson, 1987; van de Vliert & Euwema, 1994). Using Sillars's (see Chapter 2; Sillars et al., 1982; Sillars & Wilmot, 1994) scheme to classify verbal statements made during a conflict discussion, confrontive (e.g., personal criticism, hostile questions) and analytic (e.g., disclosive statements, soliciting criticism) remarks represent clear cases of conflict engagement, whereas denial and equivocation and topic management (i.e., topic shifts and topic avoidance) reflect conflict avoidance. Irreverent and conciliatory remarks fall somewhere in the middle of engagement versus nonengagement. Using Rusbult's (Rusbult & Zembrodt, 1983; Rusbult, Zembrodt, & Gunn, 1982) typology of responses to relational dissatisfaction, *exit* (e.g., threatening to leave, screaming shrewishly at one's partner) and *voice* (e.g., discussing problems, compromising) represent "active" responses, whereas *loyalty* (e.g., supporting the partner when others criticize him or her, praying for improvement) and *neglect* (e.g., ignoring the partner or spending less time together, refusing to discuss problems) entail "passive" responses.

A common interactional pattern in conflict is the demand-withdrawal sequence (e.g., Baucom, Notarius, Burnett, & Haefner, 1990; Christensen & Heavey, 1990). This sequence occurs when one partner (who desires change) seeks to engage the other person in conflict and makes demands, while the partner from whom change is sought withdraws. Although both men and women may be inclined to demand when they seek a change in their partner, men may be more inclined than women to withdraw because of their relatively higher and sustained negative arousal to conflict (e.g., Gottman, 1990; Gottman & Carrere, 1994). Besides one's physiological reaction to conflict, inequity provides an alternative explanation (Christensen & Heavey, 1990). That is, the partner who is underbenefited in a relationship would be more likely to confront (and less likely to withdraw) than would the partner who is treated equitably (as discussed in Chapter 1).

Although avoidance of particular conflicts can be constructive in relationships, failing to confront salient and important conflict issues over the long haul can be dysfunctional. For example, Gottman and Krokoff (1989) found that expression of anger was negatively correlated with concurrent relational satisfaction but was positively correlated with satisfaction measured 3 years after the interaction. It is important to recognize, however, that relative patterns of conflict avoidance or engagement will vary according to a couple's relational ideology and history. Responses to conflict issues may become relatively more passive over time (Rusbult, 1987; Zietlow & Sillars, 1988), and the ultimate effect of conflict avoidance on relational quality is moderated somewhat by relational standards and expectations held by partners (e.g., "Don't make mountains out of mole hills") (Pike & Sillars, 1985).

A second common dimension used to characterize conflict behaviors is positivity versus negativity of affect (e.g., Gottman, 1979; Sillars & Wilmot, 1994). Conflict actions are perceived to be relatively more or less disagreeable—that is, strained and unpleasant (van de Vliert & Euwema, 1994). Some verbal remarks are logically more positive in sentiment (e.g., supportive and conciliatory comments), whereas others are clearly more hostile and negative (e.g., demands, threats, and insults). However, because the verbal content of messages can be relatively neutral or ambiguous with respect to affect, nonverbal cues (i.e., facial and vocal behaviors) are more important in determining meaning.

Interestingly, the type of affect exhibited by relational partners is said to be gender related. Levenson and Gottman (1985) reported that husbands' negative affect consists largely of anger and contempt (78%), whereas wives' negative affect is comprised mostly of sadness, fear, and whining (93%). In many other ways, however, conflict behaviors of men and women in close relationships are often very similar and/or run counter to cultural sex stereotypes (Cupach & Canary, in press). In Chapter 6, we discuss more thoroughly the issue of sex differences in conflict management.

The third global feature employed to characterize conflict behavior is whether it is constructive or destructive for the parties' relationship (e.g., Deutsch, 1973; Roloff, 1976; Rusbult, 1987). Constructive behavior is assumed to be cooperative, prosocial, and relationship preserving, whereas destructive behavior is considered competitive, antisocial, and relationship undermining. Integrative conflict behavior is assumed to be constructive, and distributive behavior is assumed to be destructive for relationships. Avoidance conflict behavior can be either constructive or destructive (Fitzpatrick, Fallis, & Vance, 1982; Rands, Levinger, & Mellinger, 1981; Rusbult, 1987), depending on factors such as timing, how avoidance unfolds, what relational stand-ards are held regarding conflict engagement, and who reports the avoidance (i.e., self or partner). Clearly, a good deal of research attempts to verify empirically what particular behaviors are associated with relationship satisfaction, adjustment, and stability, and which ones predict dissatisfaction and distress. We now turn to the issue of conflict and relational quality.

ᴥ Conflict Management Behaviors and Relational Quality

Aggregates of Conflict and Outcomes

Several self-report investigations have shown an association be-tween a person's relational satisfaction and perception of one's own and partner's conflict behaviors. For example, Rands and colleagues (1981) surveyed 244 married couples and found that marital satisfac-tion was negatively associated with perceptions that the spouse en-gaged in an attacking or avoiding style of conflict management. In examining the taped discussions of married partners regarding con-flictual issues, Ting-Toomey (1983b) found marital satisfaction to be positively associated with the proportion of exhibited integrative and descriptive acts and negatively associated with the proportion of disintegrative acts.

For specific episodes of conflict in both marital and nonmarital romantic relationships, we (Canary & Cupach, 1988; Canary & Spitzberg, 1989; Spitzberg, Canary, & Cupach, 1994) have found that reported use of integrative tactics is positively associated with rela-tional satisfaction; reported use of distributive tactics is negatively associated with satisfaction. Importantly for this competence-based approach, the link between conflict and satisfaction has been dramati-cally mediated by perceptions of the communicator's competence. That is, conflict behaviors do not appear to have a direct influence on relational outcomes; rather, people first interpret conflict behaviors in terms of how appropriate and effective the partner was, and these interpretations filter the effects due to conflict behavior. The associa-tions regarding strategy-outcome links pertain both to one's own reported behavior and to behavior ascribed to one's partner.

Rusbult and colleagues (Rusbult, 1993; Rusbult, Verette, Whitney, Slovik, & Lipkus, 1991) have conducted several investigations to explain *accommodation* processes. "Accommodation refers to an individual's willingness, when a partner has engaged in a potentially destructive behavior, to (a) inhibit tendencies to react destructively in turn and (b) instead engage in constructive reactions" (Rusbult et al., 1991, p. 53). A number of factors were found to predict the likelihood of accommodation. One of the most important predictors was commitment to the relationship, which mediated the effects of many other factors. In addition, feelings of relational satisfaction had both direct and indirect (i.e., mediated through commitment) effects on accommodation tendencies.

Research on global accommodation responses to relational dissatisfaction displays results similar to those of the conflict studies. More precisely, the constructive response of voice is positively correlated with relational satisfaction, whereas the destructive responses of exit and neglect are negatively associated with satisfaction (Goodwin, 1991; Metts & Cupach, 1990; Rusbult, Johnson, & Morrow, 1986a, 1986b).

Distressed Versus Nondistressed Couples

A number of studies have established the link between conflict and relational quality by comparing the behaviors of distressed and nondistressed married couples (for reviews, see Gottman, 1994; Schaap, 1982, 1984). Distressed couples more frequently and more intensely exhibit negative behaviors compared to nondistressed couples (e.g., Billings, 1979; Birchler & Webb, 1977; Birchler, Weiss, & Vincent, 1975; Gottman, 1979, 1994; Koren, Carlton, & Shaw, 1980; Lloyd, 1990b; Markman, 1979, 1981; Raush et al., 1974; Revensdorf et al., 1984; Vincent et al., 1975). In general, those in distressed marriages are more likely to demonstrate sarcastic, critical, hostile, coercive, and rejecting behaviors (including withdrawal). Not surprisingly, such behaviors are usually less effective in resolving disagreements and produce less satisfaction with communication and the outcome of conflict discussions (e.g., Canary & Cupach, 1988; Koren et al., 1980; Newton & Burgoon, 1990b).

Nondistressed couples, relative to distressed couples, also display a higher ratio of positive behaviors (e.g., agreeing, approving, humorous, and compliant behaviors) to negative ones (Gottman & Levenson, 1992). As aggregate measures, negative behaviors (vs. positive behaviors) more consistently predict relational outcomes, such as satisfaction (Gottman, 1979; Rusbult, 1993; Schaap, 1984).

Beyond simple aggregates of behavior, distressed couples also engage in more sequences involving negative reciprocity (Billings, 1979; Gottman, 1979; Margolin & Wampold, 1981; Pike & Sillars, 1985; Ting-Toomey, 1983a) and lengthier sequences of negative reciprocity (Gottman, Markman, & Notarius, 1977; Ting-Toomey, 1983a) compared to nondistressed couples. In other words, distressed couples are more likely to respond to the negative actions of a partner with a similar negative action. Importantly, such negative "tit-for-tat" patterns are exchanged for longer periods of time, resulting in the escalation of conflict and reification of what couples consider appropriate conflict management interaction (Sillars & Wilmot, 1994). For example, Ting-Toomey (1983a) found that couples low in marital adjustment exhibited up to 10 consecutive exchanges of attack-defend and attack-attack messages (unlike adjusted couples, who engaged in very few attack exchanges). Other research has uncovered a number of different specific sequential patterns characteristic of distressed couples.

Gottman (1979), for example, found that cross-complaining sequences were common in the discussions of dissatisfied couples. Such sequences involve one partner making a complaint and the other partner following with a counter-complaint (Gottman, 1982, p. 111):

Wife: I'm tired of spending all my time on the housework. You're not doing your share.
Husband: If you used your time efficiently, you wouldn't be tired.

Ting-Toomey (1983a) and Alberts (1988) observed similar patterns of defensiveness among couples who were low in marital adjustment. Compared to high marital adjustment couples, low adjustment couples in these studies demonstrated reciprocal chains of confront-confront, confront-defend, complain-defend, and defend-complain. For example:

Husband: You look silly in that outfit. Why don't you exercise more?
Wife: You should talk—you haven't gone jogging in over a year!

Although verbal conflict patterns can distinguish distressed from nondistressed couples, nonverbal behaviors have served as better discriminators of these couples (Gottman, 1979, 1994; Gottman & Levenson, 1988; Gottman et al., 1977). This finding probably reflects the importance of affect (experienced and inferred) in conflict episodes, as well as the fact that the relational implications of messages are largely conveyed nonverbally (Newton & Burgoon, 1990a; Watzlawick, Beavin, & Jackson, 1967).

Moreover, the observed patterns of negative affect reciprocity parallel couples' patterns of physiological responses (i.e., heart rate, skin conductance, pulse transit time, and the like). Levenson and Gottman (1983) predicted "that patterned exchanges of negative affect within the dyad would activate physiological systems and produce parallel patterning of physiological responses between the spouses" (p. 588). Amazingly, physiological coupling—the interrelatedness of partners' physiological responses—during the discussion of a marital problem area accounted for 60% of the variance in marital satisfaction. Physiological coupling has also been shown to predict levels of marital satisfaction 5 years later (Levenson & Gottman, 1985). It is possible that the reciprocation of negative affect is the most relationship-damaging form of interaction in which a couple can engage.

Recently, Gottman (1994) presented his theory of marital stability that highlights conflict interaction as a primary generative mechanism. In brief, Gottman held that couples either regulate or do not regulate their conflict responses. *Regulate* refers to the ability of both partners to respond in significantly more positive than negative messages during interaction, and a nonregulated couple includes at least one partner who does not demonstrate such ability. For Gottman (see also Gottman & Levenson, 1992), a "set point" predicts whether the relationship is "balanced": Stable and satisfied couples are said to enact five times more positive than negative interaction behaviors. Hence, the 5:1 positive to negative ratio constitutes an index of being "balanced," such that couples engaging in a lower positive to negative behavior ratio risk becoming imbalanced.

Gottman (1994) has emphasized that four messages are particularly negative and lead to "cascades" of isolation and withdrawal, due to the recipient of these messages feeling "flooded" by the (unexpected) negativity. (Gottman called these behaviors the "Four Horsemen of the Apocalypse" to underscore their devastating consequences.) These interaction behaviors emerge in the following order: *complaining/criticizing* (about some features of the partner) leads to *contempt* (i.e., acting as if sickened by the partner), which in turn leads to *defensiveness* (i.e., protecting self), which leads to *stonewalling* (i.e., emotional withdrawal and refusal to participate in conversation). As Gottman showed, regulated stable couples do not engage in such a cascade, whereas unstable couples do.

Gottman also described how couples' conflict behavior discriminates them into discrete types, how negative behaviors lead to emotional "flooding" and "diffuse physiological arousal," and how men engage in more withdrawal, among other important concepts we cannot fully cover here. We wish to stress that relational maintenance is clearly linked to microscopic conflict behaviors, ones that Gottman (and others) empirically identified and theoretically elaborated.

The "demand-withdrawal" pattern, which typically refers to a pattern of wife demand followed by husband withdrawal, has been explained using other theories as well. For example, Napier (1978) identified a similar "rejection-intrusion" pattern stemming from conflicts regarding one partner's desire for autonomy and the other's wish for interdependence. Napier held that one's family of origin provides models for how such conflicts are managed.

Christensen and Heavey (1990) tested two alternative explanations for the demand-withdrawal pattern. The first explanation draws from sex role stereotypes, in which men are more independent than women and women seek more intimacy than men due to socialization processes. The second explanation derives from equity theory. This explanation assumes that because they are more often underbenefited in marriage, women are more likely to approach the spouse to repair the inequity. But because husbands enjoy more rewards than do their wives in most marriages, husbands resist changing the status quo by withdrawing from discussion of the problematic issues. Christensen and Heavey rated partner interactions on topics in which one partner sought to change the other. They reported a crossed interaction effect, where wife demand-husband withdrawal occurred most often when the woman sought change. But husband demand-wife withdrawal occurred more often than wife demand-husband withdrawal when the man wanted to change the status quo. Christensen and Heavey interpreted these findings as support for a social exchange view and not the stereotypical sex difference view (i.e., women are inherently more relationally sensitive).

Longitudinal Research

It is difficult to parse the causal links between conflict behavior and relational properties. The research is mostly nonexperimental (or quasi-experimental) and cross-sectional. Furthermore, the ties between behaviors and relational phenomena are potentially complex and reciprocal. Two longitudinal studies of marital relationships, however, address the temporal connection between conflict behavior and relational satisfaction.

Gottman and Krokoff (1989) videotaped couples while they discussed a salient conflict issue in their marriage. Observational coding of the interaction revealed a number of interesting findings. First, a different pattern of behavior predicted concurrent satisfaction than predicted changes in satisfaction 3 years later. Specifically, conflict engagement and the expression of anger were negatively associated with concurrent satisfaction but were associated with increases in satisfaction over time. The wife's expressions of contempt and anger were negatively associated with concurrent marital satisfaction for both partners but positively associated with change in her (and only her) marital satisfaction. Thus, some behaviors that seem negative at the time they are enacted may be productive in the long run.

Second, the wife's positive verbal interaction predicted concurrent marital satisfaction but was associated with deterioration of satisfaction over time. As Gottman and Krokoff (1989) indicated, "We cannot assume that, because interaction patterns correlate with concurrent relationship satisfaction, we can confidently label them 'functional' or 'dysfunctional' " (p. 51).

Third, some behaviors were consistently dysfunctional; that is, defensiveness, stubbornness, and withdrawal (especially by the husband) were associated with deterioration of marital satisfaction over time as well as concurrent distress. In addition, the husband's whining was associated with declines in his satisfaction, whereas the wife's fear predicted declines in her satisfaction. The wife's sadness predicted deterioration in satisfaction for both partners. Gottman and Krokoff (1989) summarized the implications of these complex findings:

In terms of recommendations for marriage, our results suggest that wives should confront disagreement and should not be overly compliant, fearful, and sad but should express anger and contempt. Husbands should also engage in conflict but should not be stubborn or withdrawn. Neither spouse should be defensive. (p. 51)

Noller and colleagues (Noller, Feeney, Bonnell, & Callan, 1994) assessed couples' communication and relationship satisfaction just prior to marriage and twice during the first 2 years of marriage. Both self-report and videotaped interaction data were collected.

A number of intriguing findings emerged. First, conflict patterns did not exhibit significant change over time. However, whether entrenched patterns of conflict behavior are due to the personality of one (or both) relational partner(s) or to relational systemic properties remains unclear. Second, spouses higher in satisfaction exhibited less negativity in handling conflict. In particular, they were less likely to manipulate their partner, employ threats, behave coercively, and exhibit destructive patterns such as demand-withdraw. More satisfied partners were also less likely to avoid or withdraw from conflict compared to those lower in satisfaction. Notably, conflict communication measures predicted later satisfaction for wives only. Third, relationship satisfaction predicted subsequent conflict patterns.

The strongest prediction was from relationship satisfaction assessed after a year of marriage to conflict variables after almost 2 years of marriage. Relationship satisfaction was most consistently related to later ratings of disengagement for husbands. For wives, conflict processes involving negativity, withdrawal and disengagement were predicted by earlier satisfaction. With regard to the videotaped strategies, the strongest effects were for wives' support of partner, which was predicted by both own and husbands' earlier satisfaction. (Noller et al., 1994, p. 248)

The authors concluded from these data that the connection between relationship satisfaction and conflict behavior over time is reciprocal.

❧ Factors Influencing Conflict Management

In addition to relationship quality and climate, a number of other factors potentially influence conflict behavior in any given situation.

Among these are biological sex (Berryman-Fink & Brunner, 1987); personality traits such as locus of control (Canary et al., 1988), attachment style, and need for achievement (Kilmann & Thomas, 1975; Pistole, 1989; Utley et al., 1989); general beliefs about relationships (Metts & Cupach, 1990); beliefs about conflict in particular (Crohan, 1992); and expectancies regarding the efficacy of solving relational conflicts (Fincham & Bradbury, 1987a; Weiss, 1984). However, these factors tend to be distal—that is, indirect—and rather modest in magnitude of importance, when compared to more proximal influences such as the partner's behavior (Burggraf & Sillars, 1987).

As relationships develop more of a history and unique culture, the relational milieu in which conflict occurs becomes increasingly influential (see also Chapter 6). In addition, perceptions attendant on the nature of a particular conflict situation have a potent effect on how partners manage a dispute. In the following sections, we consider how aspects of the interpersonal relationship and of the particular conflict episode itself influence and constrain conflict management. Specifically, research indicates that relational and episodic characteristics frame or contextualize the interpretation of a conflict and thereby influence its communicative management.

Relational Context for Conflict Interaction

The relational culture that couples develop over time represents an increasingly shared symbolic world that reflects the identity of the relationship and its partners. For example, Fitzpatrick (1988a) identified three general types of marriage based on a number of dimensions of married life. *Traditionals* endorse conventional ideas about marriage and family life, value partner interdependence, and prefer to confront conflict over serious issues only. *Independents* subscribe to unconventional ideas about marriage and family life, value partner autonomy as well as interdependence, and prefer direct confrontation over a wide range of conflict issues. *Separates* ambivalently support conventional ideas about marriage and family life, value partner autonomy (vs. interdependence), and prefer to avoid conflict.

Fitzpatrick (1988b) summarized several studies concerning how different marital types manage conflict. Traditionals appear to confront one another mostly over important issues, and they rely on avoidance less often than do other couple types. Moreover, Traditionals enact cooperative behaviors, such as mutual problem solving (e.g., validation and contract sequences) and appeals to the relationship (Witteman & Fitzpatrick, 1986). In addition, the emotional tone of Traditional conflicts appears to be low; they maintain neutral or positive affect during conflict (Sillars, Pike, Jones, & Redmon, 1983).

Independents appear to thrive on confrontation in conflict. In fact, research indicates that Independents are unhappy when the partner avoids the issue or when neutral affect predominates in the discussion. Independents offer and seek information, and they readily use confrontation, especially in the face of partner avoidance (Fitzpatrick, 1988b; Sillars et al., 1983). Independents are likely to engage in refutation, to discount the other person's arguments, and to seek information more than do the other types (Witteman & Fitzpatrick, 1986). Also, Independents counter dominant actions of the spouse with dominant actions of their own (Williamson & Fitzpatrick, 1985).

Separates actively avoid conflict. For example, Sillars et al. (1983) found that Separates use explicit denial to each other that there is a problem (although they had previously indicated to the researchers there was in fact a problem). Likewise, Witteman and Fitzpatrick (1986) found that Separates used "guerrilla-like" communication to persuade their partner while safeguarding their autonomy; that is, they constrained the other person's behaviors and did not seek information from one another but appealed to their partner's sense of values. When Separates do confront the partner, they do so in short segments and with an immediate escape into nonconfrontation (Fitzpatrick, 1988b).

Based entirely on their conflict interaction behaviors, Gottman (1994) has identified three functional and two dysfunctional couple types. The three functional types resemble Fitzpatrick's (1988a) types. According to Gottman, *conflict-minimizers* "are fairly flat emotionally and somewhat distant from one another" (akin to Separates) (p. 136). On the other hand, *volatile couples* "thrive on combat, and they try to influence one another about most everything. This type of couple is quite passionate and emotionally expressive. They fight a lot, but they also laugh a lot" (similar to Independents) (pp. 136-137). The third functional type, *validating couples*, parallels Traditional couples in their emotional interdependence but show neutral affect in managing conflict. Gottman indicates that two other couple types are dysfunctional and characterized by patterns of defensiveness, withdrawal, and contempt for each other.

Consistent with the observed verbal behavioral patterns, Honeycutt et al. (1993; based on Jones & Gallois, 1989) examined differences among couple types with respect to endorsement of communicative rules for managing conflict. Endorsement of four rule factors was assessed in married and engaged couples: positive understanding (e.g., should be able to say sorry, listen to other), rationality (e.g., don't get angry, don't raise voice), conciseness (e.g., should get to point quickly, be consistent), and consideration (e.g., don't make the other feel guilty, don't mimic or be sarcastic). Honeycutt et al. (1993) predicted and found that Traditionals endorsed more communicative rules (especially rationality) than did Independents. (Separates were too few in number to analyze.)

Episodic Context for Conflict Interaction

The perceptions and reactions that one has in response to a perceived conflict constitute important elements of the conflict context. Cognitions about a conflict episode play a role in determining how partners interact with each other. In turn, episodic perceptions influence the degree and sort of effect that a conflict interaction will exert on the relationship in the long run. Five perceptual factors lend insight into romantic couples' conflicts.

First, attributional activity, particularly attempts to explain the causes of behavior, seems to be especially salient during conflict, when arousal and defensiveness are heightened (Orvis et al., 1976; Sillars & Scott, 1983). Negative and unpleasant relational events stimulate more attribution making than positive and pleasant events (Holtzworth-Munroe & Jacobson, 1985, 1988). Moreover, the affective climate of a relationship likely influences the attributional tendencies of relational partners. Individuals in happy relationships make kinder attributions, whereas individuals who are dissatisfied in their relationships make malevolent judgments, especially in terms of seeing the conflict as due to global versus specific causal factors (see Bradbury & Fincham, 1990, for a review). Thus, spouses in nondistressed relationships attribute negative partner behaviors to unstable, specific, and external circumstances, whereas partners in distressed marriages view such behaviors as stable, global, and tied to the partner (e.g.,

Baucom, Sayers, & Duhe, 1989). Attributions of responsibility are similarly related to marital satisfaction. The perceived intentionality, blameworthiness, and selfish motivation of partner's behavior are negatively associated with marital satisfaction (Bradbury & Fincham, 1988; Fincham, Beach, & Nelson, 1987; Fincham & Bradbury, 1987b).

Second, such perceptions influence one's approach to managing the conflict. For example, Witteman (1988, 1992) found that attributing the cause of a problem to one's partner was associated with the tendency to employ competitive, distributive conflict behaviors (Witteman, 1988, 1992). Negative feelings toward a partner and attributions of partner intent were also associated with distributive behaviors. These findings parallel Sillars's (1980a, 1980b) research regarding roommate conflicts.

Next, goals that each partner pursues involve alternative conflict management behaviors. Witteman (1988, 1992) observed that when goals are perceived to be mutual, individuals are more likely to use integrative conflict management. Moreover, type of goal affects conflict behavior. Canary and colleagues (1988) found that when the goal was to defend a personal right, personal criticism was more likely and integrative conflict tactics were less likely to be used. When the goal was to change the relationship, however, integrative tactics were used more often.

Fourth, perceptions associated with conflict episodes also are important in the broader scheme of relationship functioning. Research by Lloyd (1987) suggests that perceived characteristics of conflict situations are linked to relational quality. Moreover, situational dimensions or characteristics that are important to women may differ from the characteristics important to men. Lloyd had seriously involved premarital couples keep diary records of disagreements over a 2-week period. For each disagreement, participants indicated various characteristics of the conflict, including intensity (high vs. low), resolution (unresolved vs. resolved), and stability (issue rarely discussed vs. issue discussed often). In addition, participants completed measures of relationship quality (i.e., love, satisfaction, and commitment) and communication quality (i.e., hostility, self-disclosure anxiety, negotiation, and manipulation).

Lloyd (1987) found that the most salient aspect of conflict in terms of relational quality was stability of the conflict issue for men and number of conflicts for women. For men, perceived stability of conflicts was associated with lower levels of love and commitment, whereas for women, the greater the number of conflicts reported, the lower the levels of love and commitment. In addition, resolution of conflict was associated with greater relationship satisfaction for women. Lloyd further discovered that these findings were moderated by who initiated the conflicts. Specifically, the stability of partner-initiated conflicts was most relevant to relationship quality for men, whereas the resolution of self-initiated conflicts was most relevant to relationship quality for women. Lloyd (1987) explains that "males who feel the same issues are brought up repeatedly by their partners also perceive lower levels of love and commitment. Females who feel that the conflicts they initiate are less resolved also perceive lower levels of love and satisfaction" (p. 292). These results suggest that men and women may tend to assume different perceptual perspectives in interpersonal conflict that can lead to undesirable cycles of women preferring to discuss unresolved issues, which men take as signs of unhappiness. In Lloyd's (1987) study, the level of resolution of self-initiated conflict was inversely associated with perceived stability of the conflict issue for women. That is, if the issue was resolved, it was not seen as a chronic problem by women. However, at the same time, men did not associate resolution with the number of times an issue was brought up by their partner.

> Picking an arbitrary starting point, the cycle becomes one of the female partner initiating a conflict repeatedly in order to get the underlying issue resolved (with resolution serving to increase her relationship quality), while at the same time the male partner's perception that she has initiated a conflict on an issue that has come up over and over serves to decrease his perceived relationship quality. (Lloyd, 1987, p. 293)

This characterization is consistent with the classic demand-withdrawal pattern of conflict management mentioned previously (Christensen & Heavey, 1990; Kelley et al., 1978).

In a follow-up study 36 months later, Lloyd (1990a) was able to discriminate the 16 couples who were still together from the 9 who had terminated their relationships. Those in noncontinuing relationships reported greater stability of conflict issues compared to those in continuing relationships. Thus, problems seem to be more persistent and recurring in troubled relationships. Lloyd also found that females in continuing relationships reported more resolution of conflicts when compared to females in noncontinuing relationships.

Finally, although factors such as *current* relational satisfaction are associated with both episode-specific perceptions and episode-specific behaviors in conflict situations, the exact causal connections defy specification given the dearth of longitudinal data on this point. Nevertheless, evidence increasingly suggests that episodic interpretations mediate the association between conflict behavior and subsequent relationship properties. Fincham and Bradbury (1987b) showed that causal and responsibility attributions for marital problems and negative spouse behaviors predicted marital satisfaction for wives (but not husbands) 12 months later.

Canary and his colleagues (Canary & Cupach, 1988; Canary & Spitzberg, 1989, 1990) have investigated the perceived communication competence of conflict behaviors as a mediating factor. Their studies consistently show that integrative conflict behaviors are perceived to be appropriate and effective (i.e., communicatively competent), whereas distributive behaviors are seen as inappropriate and ineffective. Moreover, assessments of the partner's competence mediate the link between conflict and relationship outcomes. That is, perceptions that a partner has handled conflict competently, in turn, are associated with positive relational qualities such as trust, mutuality of control, intimacy, and relational satisfaction.

❧ Conclusions

The current research on conflict in romantic relationships presents a diverse set of findings. Accordingly, generalizations about conflict in romantic relationships risk homogenization of some interesting nuances presented in the research. In light of this risk, we believe four conclusions merit exploration at this point.

First, the research suggests that conflict functions in romantic relationships as a means of negotiating important issues as well as styles of interdependence. That is, particular issues, such as who does what at home and where the couple should go for vacation, provide the content, whereas how couples manage their disagreements structures the system of interaction characterizing the relationship. This observation is certainly not new (e.g., Watzlawick et al.'s [1967] bifurcation of content and relational dimensions of communication). What is new concerns how conflict appears to play an important role in the reflection of different couple types, as the research by both Fitzpatrick and Gottman reported. In other words, people participate in the creation of different relational types largely through their conflict interaction behaviors. Three behaviors that appear to distinguish among couple types are length of confrontation, avoidance or withdrawal, and distributive tactics. For example, Separates use explicit avoidance, short spurts of confrontation, and controlling forms of distributive behaviors; Independents engage in indirect forms of avoidance, confrontation, and some distributive behaviors.

Second, the finding that negativity and reciprocation of negative affect are detrimental to relationships emerges most clearly in the marital interaction literature. Here we find alternative, microscopic ways that negativity occurs during interaction. Gottman (1994) has isolated four forms of negativity—which he calls the "Four Horsemen of the Apocalypse" to underscore their devastating consequences. Gottman has shown that these evolve in the following order, representing a "cascade" of isolation and withdrawal: complaining/criticizing leads to contempt, which leads to defensiveness, which leads to stonewalling. As Gottman observed, stable couples do not engage in such a cascade, whereas unstable couples do. Of course, other researchers have found similar patterns of negative couple interaction that sketch a portrait of dissatisfaction and withdrawal (e.g., Raush et al., 1974; Sillars & Wilmot, 1994; Ting-Toomey, 1983a).

Some negative conflict is to be expected in any romantic involvement, but its continued use will corrode the relationship. Given both the tendency for couples to reciprocate behaviors and the tendency for dysfunctional couples to become enmeshed over several exchanges in reciprocation of negativity, the following conclusion clearly is warranted: One should resist the temptation to reciprocate negativity with either negativity or stonewalling over time. According to most research, frequent use and reciprocation of negative interaction behaviors erode romantic involvements, whereas direct and cooperative engagement over the issues does not.

Third, couples translate interaction sequences into inferences about the nature of the relationship. Conflicts can appear isolated, atypical, and external to the couple, or they can be seen as reflecting ongoing, typical problems internal to the couple. As documented above, dissatisfied couples attribute their problems to global, stable, and internal features of the partner. Also, recall that dissatisfied couples enact patterns of negativity, which are likewise attributed to global, stable, and internal properties of the partner or the relationship. In other words, it appears that both processes of interaction as well as problems outlined during interaction lead people to assess their associations in relationship-enhancing or -debasing terms. On a similar point, Gottman (1994) concluded that

> as couples continue to feel flooded [due to partner negativity] and increase the emotional distance between them, this is reflected in their cognitions about the entire marriage and its history, and not just particular kinds of interactions. The process of reacting to a partner's negative emotional expressions in one instance and then entering the distance and isolation cascade is a process of increasing globality in how one thinks of the marriage. (p. 358)

Conflict causes that are attributed to global, stable, internal, and intentional features of the partner appear to be quite difficult to change and may even provide justification for use of negative behavior. People adopt attributions precisely because they provide a means of interpreting the partner's behaviors. Changing such attributions may very likely require cognitive restructuring or couple counseling to learn how to punctuate and interpret each other's behavior in different ways, using different schemes (Gottman, 1994; Robin & Foster, 1989; Watzlawick et al., 1967). Of course, one irony concerns how both partners in a dissatisfied relationship tend to attribute conflict behaviors and causes to each other, and this probably often occurs simultaneously. But given that people focus externally on the other more than on self (Storms, 1973; cf. Christensen et al., 1983), the irony escapes most partners. That is, they see the partner's whining or sarcasm but not their own; hence, their sense making of the event in terms of global, stable, and internal attributions appears to be founded on some very solid empirical data. Over time, these data become empirical generalizations of a lawlike nature. Another reason that people find difficulty revising unkind attributions stems from their function as self-preserving. That is, people probably believe that they are better prepared to protect themselves by hanging on to such attributions (e.g., "She is inconsiderate, rude, and arrogant to talk to me like that. I'll show her who is in charge.").

Finally, negative behaviors clearly harm the welfare of the relationship—it appears that psychological withdrawal reflected in conversational stonewalling also precludes people from managing their conflicts in relationally enhancing ways. At least two types of avoidance have emerged in the literature—one type is blatant, direct, and controlling; the other type is subtle, indirect, and disengaging (e.g., Fitzpatrick, 1988b). The first avoidance type, which is labeled *stonewalling* (Gottman, 1994), comes off as offensive as it seeks to destroy information and emotional exchange. The second type, which is referred to as *distraction*, indicates a defensive posture, to shift the issue or to make light of the discussion but without neglecting the partner in the process. Continued examination of these types of avoidance appears to be an important research issue.

6

Conclusions About and Prospects for Research on Conflict in Close Relationships

W e have arrived at the point where we want to present conclusions about conflict processes in close, personal relationships.
As we reviewed the research, we were impressed by what remains to
be known as well as what we already know. The many studies on
interpersonal conflict support several conclusions yet they simultaneously point to future directions. We offer conclusions first, followed
by suggestions for specific areas of continued research efforts.

⸙ Conclusions About Conflict and . . .

Our conclusions concern four points of connection: (a) links between interpersonal conflict and personal development, (b) ties between conflict and development of close relationships, (c) associations

between relational maintenance and types of conflict interactions, and (d) ways in which conflict behavior reflects sex differences. We discuss each in turn.

Conflict and Personal Development

Perhaps more than any other type of interaction, conflict acts as a catalyst for personal development. For example, babies learn (in terms of social learning theory) how to control undesired parental behaviors (Patterson, 1979)—for example, to cry until the parent pays attention. Through thousands of hours of conversation with mothers and young peers, toddlers learn how to apply particular kinds of argument to different conflict topics (Dunn & Munn, 1985, 1987). As social perspective taking skills increase, children learn that conflict topics are multilayered, that disagreement episodes involve psychological as well as physical features, and that they themselves are members of an interdependent relational system that naturally entails conflict as a method of coordination.

Adolescents express their physical and psychological growth during puberty through different conflict behaviors for different issues than they did as children. As Smetana (1989) has shown, adolescents seek to establish rights for personal control, especially in terms of personal appearance, habits, and friends. They reject parental authority over these issues, which naturally plays out in a series of conflict episodes. Importantly, the mother often loses power in the wake of her adolescent child's assertiveness (Steinberg, 1987). And, according to Robin and Foster (1989), conflict encounters are essential for the continuation of the family system: Perpetuation of the family system will cease unless the adolescent asserts him- or herself. The same cycle of development and issues under contention transfer to the next generation as the young adult begins his or her own family.

This prototypical model of personal development is qualified by the manner in which parents directly and indirectly "teach" children conflict interaction behaviors. In the United States, a full half of marriages end in divorce (Attridge, 1994), and most U.S. families do not conform to the "Standard North American Family" (i.e., both parents, legally married, under the same roof; Peck, 1988; Smith, 1993). This implies that the prototypical traditional model of marriage—and its corresponding "family values"—does not exist for most children. Instead, children will likely learn conflict interactions from one parent and observe difficult negotiations involving separated or divorced parents.

The research is clear that separation or divorce *per se* does not necessarily lead to children's adjustment problems, including poor conflict management. Instead, how the parents manage their own marital and separation problems more strongly affects the children (Amato & Keith, 1991; Emery, 1982, 1992). If parents are cooperative and if at least one of them provides support for the child, then the child should develop in a normal manner. But if parents use distributive conflict behaviors, seek to compete for the child's loyalty, and do not nurture the child, then adjustment problems will likely ensue. In addition, parental incompetence at managing conflict probably leads to physical aggression or neglect of the child, which can be transferred to the child's own family years later (Minuchin, 1992).

Conflict and Relationship Development

We think the research literature, and especially that concerned with romantic types, provides three observations about the role of conflict in the development of close relationships. First, relationships and conflict interactions reciprocally frame one another. In other words, particular conflict episodes between partners on the one hand, and the relationship constructed and shared between partners on the other hand, mutually shape and constrain each other. The definition of a close relationship in terms of characteristics, such as knowledge of the other, trust, and satisfaction, affects how conflicts are created, construed, and managed. At the same time, the manner in which relational partners address conflict, both psychologically and behaviorally, influences the character of the partners' relationship. In short, the literature reveals that healthy and satisfying relationships promote constructive conflict attributions and behaviors, and constructive conflict management fosters the development of intimacy and relational stability (points on which we elaborate in the next section).

Although conflict behavior and relationship development are connected, it is not always clear empirically when conflict represents a symptom of relationship difficulty versus when conflict contributes to the formation of a relationship. Braiker and Kelley (1979) observe the difficulty in discerning the "net effect of conflict on courtship and marriage relations":

> Open conflict undoubtedly reflects factors that make unlikely the development of a cohesive and satisfying relationship; for example, the inability of one person to provide appropriate rewards for the other; or one partner's propensities and preferences to act in ways that are aversive to the other. Moreover, the continued occurrence of unresolved conflict reflects a failure of one or both partners to change or modify maladaptive behavior. Thus, open conflict is partly a symptom of causal factors that prevent relationship happiness. However, open conflict also serves to contribute to unhappiness and instability. . . . Conflict behavior itself becomes an object of conflict. The way two persons fight and the interpretations they place on each other's conflict actions often afford further reasons for unhappiness. (p. 164)

Along this line of thought, conflict and its management *reflect* the developmental course of the relationship in which they are embedded. For example, as noted in Chapter 5, conflict in the first years of marriage differs from conflict later in life in that young couples engage each other more directly as compared to middle-aged couples, who are in turn more direct than are elderly couples (Levenson et al., 1994; Zietlow & Sillars, 1988).

Second, and complementing the point just made, as relational partners become closer (with "closeness" highest in the first year of marriage), the *potential* for interpersonal conflict increases (Braiker & Kelley, 1979). Scientific definitions of intimacy involve mutual knowledge, high frequency of interaction, and intense interdependence (Perlman & Fehr, 1987). Norms of politeness and ingratiation exhibited during interaction early in the relationship give way to more intimate and risky self-disclosure and assertiveness as the relationship progresses (Braiker & Kelley, 1979). Furthermore, as relationships develop bonds of cohesion and commitment, they can more easily withstand belligerent and manipulative forms of influence during conflict episodes (Fitzpatrick & Winke, 1979).

A corollary to the observation that intimacy promotes conflict is that conflict and relational satisfaction are not incompatible. Indeed, as the research in parent-child, friendship, and romantic relationships shows, the simple frequency of conflict says relatively little about the quality of the relationship shared by partners (e.g., Raush et al., 1974). The frequency of conflict in marital relationships, for example, may be uncorrelated with relational satisfaction (e.g., Argyle & Furnham, 1983). When disagreement frequency is tied to relationship disruption (i.e., separation, divorce), it is accompanied by avoidance of confrontation and conflict negativity (e.g., McGonagle et al., 1993). It appears that in most close relationship forms, the amount of closeness and interdependence is relatively independent of the frequency of open conflict (e.g., Braiker & Kelley, 1979). This suggests several things: (a) that conflict frequency provides a weak index of relational intimacy/ adjustment, (b) that conflict frequency is less important than how conflict is managed, and (c) that couples might develop modes of managing disagreements distinct from modes enacted in other types of interactions (such as self-disclosing).

Third, perceptual accuracy regarding conflict issues is not always positive, despite an ideology of intimacy that many presume should accompany relational development (Parks, 1982). According to popular magazines, popular books (e.g., Tannen, 1990), and some research literature, partners should communicate for shared understanding of each other. Although shared understanding has been linked to positive outcomes in the past (e.g., Lewis & Spanier, 1979), knowing precisely where one's partner differs on important and problematic issues appears to be *inversely linked* to relational quality.

Using observational design and postdiscussion interviews, Sillars and colleagues (Sillars et al., 1984; Sillars et al., 1990) found that understanding areas of disagreement correlates negatively or randomly with relational satisfaction. In addition, these studies (which controlled for projection of agreement on issues) found that understanding was positively linked to negative verbal tactics and negative affect. For example, understanding one's spouse was positively associated with the spouse's use of a negative vocal tone and the spouse's use of such tactics as rejecting the partner, presumptive attributions (i.e., mind reading), and hostile questions. Sillars et al. (1984, 1990) did find that perceived agreement, not actual agreement or understanding, was positively tied to relational satisfaction. However, given that these studies are the first to control for projection of agreement, further research is required before strong inferences can be made. Nevertheless, at the minimum, this research challenges the assumption that communicating for shared understanding promotes relational welfare (cf. Knudson et al., 1980). Instead, it suggests that underscoring one's positions during conflict with negativity may increase understanding, at the sacrifice of relational quality, whereas assuming agreement can promote relational functioning.

Conflict and Relational Maintenance

Interpersonal conflict not only reciprocally frames relational development, it also functions to maintain or to erode those relationships. As Gottman (1994) indicated, the links between conflict behaviors and relational maintenance are important and nonobvious. We would be remiss if we did not underscore some of these associations.

First, research uniformly indicates that negative, distributive behaviors are enacted more by distressed/dissatisfied partners than by nondistressed/satisfied partners. Research in parent-child (e.g., Prinz et al., 1979) and romantic relationships (e.g., Schaap, 1984) clearly verifies this claim. In addition, the number of positive behaviors may also discriminate distressed from nondistressed couples or, as Gottman and Levenson (1992) suggest, the ratio of positive to negative behaviors indicates a "regulated" relationship. Of course, the definition of what comprises a "negative" conflict behavior varies across studies. Still, there is strong evidence that the following conflict behaviors damage relationships: sarcasm, negative mind reading, personal criticism, whining, contempt, disgust, and withdrawal. Gottman and Levenson (1992) found support for a "cascade" model of conflict, in which negative behaviors lead to negative attributions about the relationship, which lead to dissatisfaction and thoughts about separation. Surprisingly, demonstrations of anger are not as corrosive as withdrawal.

Second, negative responses escalate interpersonal conflicts, resembling what Wilmot (1987) called a "regressive spiral." In systems language, negative responses most often entail complementary behaviors—and these can be either symmetrical or asymmetrical (Sillars & Wilmot, 1994). For example, a person can respond negatively to a personal criticism with a complementary response, which could entail a quid pro quo personal attack (symmetrical response) or defense of self (asymmetrical response), as Ting-Toomey (1983a) found.

The reciprocation of negative affect not only damages one's assessment of the immediate conflict episode, it can also damage the relationship. In addition, reciprocations of negative affect probably occur when at least one partner relies on negative attributions to explain the conflict (Sillars, 1980b). Unfortunately, reciprocations of negative affect provide clear data to the parties that reinforce their negative attributions, thus validating that the only "realistic" approach to managing conflict is a negative or avoidant one. As mentioned, attributions about the causes of particular conflict will, over time, generalize more broadly to attributions about the partner and the relationship (Gottman, 1994). The tendency to complement negative behaviors during conflict also spills over into other supposedly "nonconflict" conversations. Accordingly, the regressive spiral that begins in conflictual situations affects perceptions of the partner and potentially contaminates any other interaction.

One response to a partner's distributive behavior is withdrawal. But when one partner eagerly wants to discuss some issue, withdrawal does not defuse the problem as much as it increases the partner's desire to discuss the issue and decreases relational satisfaction. As Christensen and Heavey (1990) have shown, such demand-withdrawal patterns can be explained according to equity theory—whoever is underbenefited is more likely to demand change. In most romantic involvements, the woman appears to be more underbenefited, which explains the sex difference for the commonly cited wife demand-husband withdrawal pattern.

The tendency to complement negative affect appears to be the strongest predictor of conflict behavior, as Sillars's research has shown. Likewise, Kiecolt-Glaser et al. (1993) reported a correlation of .74 between marital partners' negative conflict behavior. Such complementarity of negativity both constrains and empowers social actors in their ability to direct the course of conflict interactions. People who can break through the cognitive constraints of negative attributions and the behavioral constraints of negative partner behavior by enacting integrative behaviors may unilaterally alter the path of a regressive spiral. We acknowledge that many couples, in order to break out of such self-fulfilling thoughts and actions, require cognitive and/or behavioral therapy intervention. In addition, some issues constitute bedrock concerns that neither partner will negotiate, and the path to conflict resolution needs to include change in other domains of behavior (such as performing one's fair share of household chores; Gottman & Carrere, 1994). Still, being aware of the debilitating effects of negative conflict behavior may help some couples initiate more relationally promoting messages.

Research on conflict also reinforces other recent research on the ways couples maintain their close relationships. For example, Roloff and Cloven (1994) noted that dysfunctional couples can sustain otherwise troubled associations by using strategies of *retribution* (for a negative behavior), *reformulation* (of partners' negative behavior), *prevention* (mostly through avoidance), *minimization* (or discounting partners' negative behavior), and *relational justification* (or focusing on reasons to remain in the relationship). On the other hand, Stafford and Canary (1991; Canary & Stafford, 1992) have offered a set of proactive and constructive strategies that couples enact in rewarding and equitable relationships. These include *positivity* (being cheerful and avoiding criticism), *openness* (or directly discussing goals for the relationship), *assurances* (stressing one's commitment), *social networks* (or involving close friends and family in shared activities), and *sharing tasks* (doing one's fair share of household chores). These two sets of relational maintenance activities not only depict radically different processes, but they also suggest alternative routine ways couples manage to define who they are to each other. We believe these general maintenance strategies overlap with conflict orientations in different relational types.

Sex Differences in Conflict Behaviors

For many researchers, the issue of whether or not sex differences exist is moot: No study, and especially the study of marital interaction, is complete without an examination of sex differences (i.e., differences due to one's biological sex). We do not share in that assumption. Instead, we look on sex differences as a variable that should be argued as theoretically important to the particular research issue under scrutiny.

A recent summary of meta-analyses on sex differences relevant to interaction calculated that only 1% of the variance in social behavior is due to sex differences (Canary & Hause, 1993). In a meta-analysis on studies examining interpersonal communication in organizational contexts (not reviewed by Canary and Hause), Wilkins and Andersen (1991) found less than .5% (one half of 1%) of the variance was accounted for by sex differences. Wilkins and Andersen concluded, "No meaningful gender differences in positive affect behavior, influence strategies, autocratic behavior, democratic behavior, communication facilitation, and leader emergence were found" (p. 27). Canary and Hause argued that researchers too often rely on sex stereotypes, which do little to explain social behavior and, more often than not, muddle the issue. Of course, others had made the same point previously (e.g., Ragan, 1989). Nevertheless, the blinders of sex-stereotypic thinking remain firmly in place for many researchers.

Deaux and Lewis (1984) noted that women are stereotypically considered to be kind, nurturing, relationally sensitive, warm, and expressive, whereas men are stereotypically seen as dynamic, assertive, competitive, task oriented (or agenic), and competent. Many people further assume that people engage in different conflict behaviors that reflect these stereotypes. The reasoning is that, "due to socialization," men will be assertive and women will be affiliative. But such reasoning offers little beyond the tautological statement, "Men and women are different because they are different" (Deaux & Major, 1990, p. 90). The conflict research indicates a much more complex process at work. For example, although Schaap et al. (1988) found some support for sex-stereotypic behaviors during conflict, they concluded:

> All in all, we think that self-report and observational research supports the following statement. Women tend to be more emotional and show more negative affect, while men are inclined to be more rational and withdrawn. However, whatever sex differences may exist in communication, they will be affected by (a) the level or type of conflict, and (b) the couple's marital satisfaction scores. (p. 236)

We (Cupach & Canary, in press) found little support for sex-stereotypic ways of communicating during conflict interactions. Instead, in close relationships, women tend to be more assertive than men, and women use a wider range of negative behaviors, both of which are most evident in the observational literature. In addition, women use tears more but as a means of expressing anger and not acquiescence. In both survey and observational studies, we discovered more similarities than differences between men's and women's conflict behaviors. Differences that do correspond to sex stereotypes emerge most in self-report studies completed by college students, which implies that they probably impose stereotypical understanding of social behavior that is removed from actual interaction. When effects due to sex are examined in conjunction with effects due to the partner's conflict behavior, effects due to sex are virtually wiped out (Burggraf & Sillars, 1987; Dindia, 1987; Fisher, 1983).

Researchers do not need to rely on sex stereotypes. For example, Gottman and Levenson have presented impressive information concerning the physiological responses that men and women have during conflict (Gottman, 1990, 1994; Levenson et al., 1994; Levenson & Gottman, 1985). The primary finding is that, during intense interactions (and certainly during conflict), men experience more negative arousal that takes longer periods to dissipate. Such arousal stems from different social experiences during childhood, in which women become accustomed to managing relational issues and men become adept at activities, such as sports (Gottman & Carrere, 1994). The impact for conflict management behavior appears to be rather straightforward—men are more likely to withdraw, and women are more likely to pursue talk. However, the effect sizes for these findings tend to be very modest (e.g., about 4% of variance in physiological arousal was due to sex in Levenson et al., 1994). In addition, recall that the wife demand-husband withdrawal pattern is probably moderated by the issue of equity. Nevertheless, more research on how sex differences are transformed by interaction—that is, how partners negotiate their gender identity with each other over time—would complement this line of research.

ᴥ Conclusions About Future Research Prospects and Priorities

Finally, we want to address the issue of future directions, recognizing that we do not speak for any particular research group except our own and that we have invoked the fine efforts of many. We consider these to be not only specific areas for investigation but also priorities needed to direct systematic and interdisciplinary study in the area of close relationships. The future directions involve interpersonal conflict and (a) its relation to physical health; (b) salient personality factors, including competitiveness orientations; (c) nonobvious message forms; and (d) adult relationships (in addition to marital relationships and including intercultural relationships).

Conflict and Health

Researchers have recently uncovered some very intriguing information relevant to the effects of interpersonal conflict on personal health. Levenson et al. (1994) found that indexes of physiological arousal are linked to conflict. For example, husband general somatic activity was positively associated with conflict discussion, whereas husband finger pulse amplitude was negatively associated with conflict discussion. The authors linked their findings to others that showed that men tend to be more aware than women of such physiological changes and that men withdraw from conflict to reduce states of negative flooding. Women, less aware of their negative arousal and more keen on discussing relational difficulties, persist in their conflict messages. Levenson et al. concluded,

> If sustained autonomic arousal is accepted as playing a role in the etiology of disease, then the health of women would be expected to suffer most in the most unhappy marriages, which are the marriages most likely to have intractable problems and repeated bouts of high-level conflict. (p. 66)

Two recent studies provide some support for this speculation. These studies on conflict interactions of 90 newlywed couples indicate that negative conflict behaviors adversely affect blood pressure and immune systems (Kiecolt-Glaser et al., 1993) and negative conflict significantly increases pituitary and adrenal hormones (Marlarkey, Kiecolt-Glaser, Perl, & Glaser, 1994). Kiecolt-Glaser et al. and Marlarkey et al. operationalized negative conflict behaviors as "active" negativity, that is, MICS codes of criticize, disagree, deny responsibility, negative mind reading, put down, and so on, and, in Kiecolt-Glaser et al., withdrawal. To control for spurious factors, researchers selected the 90 newlywed couples because of their excellent mental health (e.g., no depression history) and physical wellness (e.g., no drug abuse). In addition, these couples tended to be very happy in their marriages. They completed a battery of measures and were sampled for blood before, during, and after a 30-minute discussion over problematic issues.

Although Kiecolt-Glaser et al. obtained blood pressure immediately following the discussion, the immunological system data were taken about 20 hours after the conflict discussion. The Kiecolt-Glaser

et al. study clearly showed that negative conflict messages immediately affect one's physical health and that the effects persist for at least
a day. If couples become habitual users of negative conflict messages,
the long-term effects of such conflict on health could be very damag-
ing. Interestingly, women appeared to suffer more health damage
than men, although the women engaged in more negativity than did
their spouses. However, the relationship between health and conflict
is probably very complex, and certain types of people might engage
in conflict with less health risk than others. This latter suggestion
relates to a second avenue for future research.

Salient Individual Factors: Locus of Control,
Argumentativeness, and Competitiveness Orientations

To emphasize how conflict becomes manifest in different types of
close relationships, we have understated the role of individual differences. Such understatement does not mean these are unimportant,
however. Some people appear to welcome conflict—or at least not be
shaken by it as much as other people appear to be. In this light, three
individual difference factors are implicated in the conflict literature
but have only been researched in conflict settings at a cursory level.
These factors could be explored more to indicate further individual
difference effects on conflict in close relationships.

Locus of Control. Locus of control refers to domain-specific attributions and expectations tied to one's personal successes and failures
(for a review, see Lefcourt, 1982). In other words, in various domains
of life, such as health, politics, and even personal relationships, people
believe that their outcomes are due primarily to their own ability and
efforts (i.e., internal locus of control) or that outcomes are due to other
people, chance, or the immediate situation (i.e., external locus of
control). Research has shown consistent, though modest, correlations
between internal locus of control for relationships and relational
harmony (e.g., Miller, Lefcourt, Holmes, Ware, & Saleh, 1986). According to this research, people who hold that relational problems can be
worked out if they applied their energies to resolve the problems are
more likely to experience positive relational outcomes.

Conflict locus of control specifically has been found to correlate
with conflict behaviors more powerfully than did a general locus-of-

control orientation (Canary et al., 1988). That is, people vary in the extent to which they believe that their conflict outcomes are due mostly to their own ability and effort (an internal conflict locus of control) or that conflict outcomes are primarily due to the partner or chance (an external conflict locus of control). Canary et al. (1988) reported that integrative conflict behaviors were positively associated with internality, whereas distributive and avoidant behaviors were positively associated with externality.

In two relevant studies, Fincham and Bradbury (1987a) tested Doherty's (1981) notion of *efficacy* as it relates to attributions of conflict causes. According to Doherty (1981), efficacy references the extent to which one person or a couple believes that they can solve their problems. Consistent with expectations, efficacy was negatively associated with beliefs that the other person was responsible for the conflict, and (in Study 2) efficacy was negatively tied to perceived stability of conflict. In sum, it appears that one's internality and efficacy beliefs lead to proactive and productive conflict management attributions and behaviors.

Linking attributions, locus of control, perceived efficacy, and behavior in particular conflicts should reveal much about self-control in the face of emotional relational discussions. More important from a theoretical perspective, such an approach suggests one way cognitions are transformed into behaviors during conflict episodes. People assess the underlying causes for the conflict, assess their own ability and required effort to manage the situation effectively, and then act in ways consistent with these assessments.

Argumentativeness. Infante and colleagues proposed that people vary in their desire to engage in argument activities, or in their *argumentativeness* (Infante, 1987; Infante & Rancer, 1982). Most critically, Infante and colleagues have provided initial evidence that argumentativeness functions to promote healthy conflict interactions. Their reasoning and results indicate that a proclivity for engaging in fair fighting preempts aggressive attacks on the person (e.g., Infante, 1987; Infante et al., 1989).

Unfortunately, no observational studies have been published on the interaction behaviors of people who vary in their argumentativeness, which indicates that similar paper-and-pencil methods constitute the mass of data on the construct. Thus, we cannot specify the behavioral correlates of argumentativeness, especially with respect to ongoing problems within close relationships. For example, no observational research has, to our knowledge, revealed if highly argumentative people (vs. low argumentative counterparts) in fact engage in *longer* discussions and/or less intense ones when issues under contention remain unresolved. Furthermore, as we indicated earlier in this chapter, the closer (i.e., more intimate and interdependent) the relationship becomes, the more it affects and reflects conflict behavior. Hence, although the initial evidence for the importance of this construct has been provided, future research must still pinpoint how conflict behaviors in close involvements vary as a function of argumentativeness.

Competitiveness/Type A Pattern. *Competitiveness* has been defined most often (in opposition to cooperativeness) as the desire to achieve one's goals independently or at the cost of another's goals (Deutsch, 1949). Competitiveness is generally considered a negative influence on conflict behavior as well as relationships. For example, James and Johnson (1987) argued that a competitive orientation is "antithetical" to personal relationships. In addition, in a study of competition between college-aged romantic partners, Messman and Mikesell (1994) found moderate correlations (.30 to .51) between areas of competition (e.g., competing for recognition, competing at games) and self-reported competitive conflict behaviors (e.g., shout at partner, show that I lost my temper, etc.).

Research into the Type A behavior pattern, of which competitiveness is a central feature, provides further direction for conflict research. Friedman and Rosenman (1974) described the Type A pattern as consisting of three issues: extreme competitiveness, time urgency, and aggression/hostility. Matthews (1982) further noted that Type A does not connote a trait but rather a complex of traits and behavioral responses linked to certain situations that specifically appear to predict coronary heart disease (CHD) as well as psychological and social phenomena (for a review, see Matthews, 1982).

In terms of conflict-related approaches, several researchers explore how Type A individuals differ from Type B individuals (i.e., people who display an absence of the Type A behaviors). Carver and Glass (1978) observed more aggressive behaviors enacted by Type A males than by Type B males in situations involving a frustrating task. Rosenberger and Strube (1986) argued that a Type A person's controlling and competitive orientations impede relational harmony. These authors found, in heterosexual dating pairs, that if the female was Type A, the couple's perceptions of relational satisfaction and stability were lower than in couples with Type B females. Last, Van Egeren (1979) found that when individuals were paired with similar others, Type As were more aggressive and competitive than were Type Bs. However, when a Type A person was paired with a Type B person, significant variations between people of different types virtually disappeared.

The Type A behavior pattern is linked clearly to conflict-relevant issues such as aggression and desire for dominance and control. A promising next step would be to observe individuals in close relationships who vary in terms of the Type A pattern to see how their competitiveness, aggression, and impatience associate with conflict emergence and engagement.

Nonobvious Conflict Messages

Some readers may feel underwhelmed by interpersonal conflict research because many of the findings appear overly obvious. For example, that positive messages promote kind attributions and relational quality (whereas negative conflict behaviors adversely affect episodic and relational outcomes) may be numbingly self-evident. And even the most precise accounts may not be insightful but rather indicate little more than validation for the presupposition that unhappy couples act unhappy.

Let us suppose for a moment that much conflict research is overly obvious. Consider the implication of this claim for future research. In our view, much good could arise at taking this charge seriously and examining nonobvious conflict behaviors. This means, at a minimum, not collapsing conflict behaviors into highly valenced categories, such as positive/negative, integrative/distributive, cooperative/competitive, affirming/disconfirming, and the like. The probability of finding significant differences between happy and unhappy couples is close to 100%. Seeking subtle forms of conflict should help to yield more insightful information.

The Nuances of Conflict Avoidance. Conflict avoidance represents an especially perplexing and intriguing aspect of conflict. Understanding the avoidance of conflict is integral to understanding the occurrence of conflict. We also recognize that conflict avoidance does not mean an absence of disagreement. McGonagle et al. (1993) reported that frequency of marital disagreement was *positively* associated with avoidance of disagreements. Indeed, the couples most prone to marital disruption over a 3-year period reported the most avoidance of disagreements *and* the highest frequency of disagreements.

However, among all behaviors identified in conflict situations, people may experience the most trouble discerning avoidance acts. For one thing, although avoidance is not necessarily enacted passively, it is often subtle and therefore more difficult to observe than forms of conciliation or confrontation. By definition, if one person succeeds in avoiding conflict, the partner will not even realize that the issue was averted.

In addition, conflict avoidance behaviors are typically more ambiguous in meaning compared to confrontation behaviors. The meaning of any behavior is inherently tied to its context. Accordingly, forms of avoidance behavior are particularly difficult for an outside observer to determine. Research shows that avoidance can be either functional or dysfunctional for a relationship, depending on how it is manifested and what the shared relational norms dictate (Fitzpatrick et al., 1982; Pike & Sillars, 1985; Rands et al., 1981; Raush et al., 1974). An irrelevant joke during a heated conflict discussion may be intended (or taken) as a constructive move to defuse an escalating situation. However, the same joke may be taken as sarcasm and may lead to further escalation of the conflict. The ambiguity of avoidance explains why research regarding its consequences seems equivocal.

Another complicating factor is that the term *avoidance* itself is rather ambiguous. It refers to a broad spectrum of phenomena that defies homogenization. Researchers employ different notions of avoidance in different investigations, making it hazardous to compare findings across studies. Consider the following ways in which avoidance can be defined/manifested:

1. Consciously withholding a particular complaint or disagreement because confrontation would be relatively more costly
2. Evading a partner's attempt to raise a particular conflictual issue at a particular time and place (e.g., changing the subject, distracting the partner)

3. Acquiescing to a partner's demands
4. Defensively withdrawing from an escalated conflict episode (e.g., walking out, stonewalling)
5. Repeatedly dodging the discussion of an area of disagreement over time
6. Changing one's own expectations so that an issue that could be conflictual becomes a nonissue (e.g., rationalizing that a partner's annoying behavior really is not annoying)
7. Systematically withdrawing from interactions with a partner (and hence withdrawing from the relationship) to preclude confrontations of any kind

Clearly, avoidance entails a number of different meanings, for relational partners and researchers alike. To comprehend conflict behavior clearly, future work should distinguish among these diverse senses of avoidance.

It also seems worthwhile to explore in greater depth various manifestations of conflict avoidance. For example, when we say that an individual is engaging in avoidance, we must ask, avoidance of what? A particular issue? Disagreement in general? Interaction involving certain "negative" behaviors exhibited by a partner (e.g., yelling, sarcasm)? Importantly, we should investigate how avoidance is "recognized." What behaviors lead one to perceive that a partner is being avoidant? What are the uses and consequences, intended and unintended, of avoidance? Is avoidance employed sometimes to intentionally escalate a conflict? When and how does avoidance backfire—that is, when does withdrawal intended to quell conflict actually exacerbate it? When is perceived evasion resented or appreciated? Such questions as these offer fertile ground for research that could provide insights about interpersonal conflict management.

Chilling Effect. One nonobvious element of interpersonal conflict relevant to avoidance concerns the "chilling effect." Roloff and Cloven (1990, 1994; Cloven & Roloff, 1993) described how partners who feel low in power withhold discussion of issues with their partner for fear of retaliation. Cloven and Roloff (1993) reported that the number of unexpressed irritations a person had about a dating partner was negatively associated with commitment ($r = -.41$) and positively associated with freedom to date others ($r = .31$). These data indicate that not communicating complaints may reflect an "exit" approach, when desirable alternatives are available and one's commitment is low (Rusbult, 1987; Rusbult et al., 1986a). The chilling effect can also reflect a "loyalty" approach, if alternatives do not exist and one's commitment is high.

Cloven and Roloff (1993) found that withheld complaints, specifically about the partner's controlling behaviors (e.g., being manipulative, getting his or her own way, being bossy), were positively correlated with perceived likelihood of being verbally or physically abused (measured according to Straus's [1979] Conflict Tactics Scale). In addition, the chilling effect operated in different ways, depending on one's levels of relational alternatives and commitment to the relationship (Roloff & Cloven, 1990).

The implication of this research is that what is *not* said presents an important topic with relational implications for conflict research. Moreover, the issue of how a partner detects the chilling effect, and what happens following such detection, needs further scrutiny.

Precise Nonverbal Behaviors. Gottman (1979) has documented that negative versus positive nonverbal displays most successfully identify satisfied and dissatisfied spouses. Similarly, Newton and Burgoon (1990a) found that nonverbal indexes of interaction involvement and cooperation powerfully affected relational outcomes, more than did verbal behaviors. Such studies underscore how important nonverbal manifestations of conflict are to relational success. If one seeks to differentiate satisfied from dissatisfied couples, then coding nonverbal messages for their valence appears to be necessary. We also believe that more needs to be done to identify precise, microscopic nonverbal conflict behaviors.

The limited research on nonverbal correlates of conflict behavior indicates that speech duration, rate, volume, and gestures can provide precise indexes of integrative, distributive, and avoidant approaches. For example, recall that Sillars et al. (1982) found that speech productivity and length of eye gaze were positively associated with cooperative, integrative tactics, whereas glancing about was negatively associated with integrative behaviors, and distributive behaviors occurred in "short bursts." We suspect that other subtle forms of nonverbal messages convey mountains of meaning during conflict. It is also likely that these subtle nonverbal conflict messages are understood to a fuller extent by relational partners in conflict than by researchers. Precise nonverbal conflict messages offer wide and deep resources for future research in close relationships.

Undeveloped Persons, Unacknowledged Relationships, and Uncharted Territory

We conclude this book by stressing one more time that we know very little about how individual development after puberty connects to variations in interpersonal conflict behavior. Accordingly, many interesting questions about adult lives and relational choices remain unexamined, implying that people over the age of 21 think and act alike during conflict in their personal relationships. There are exceptions, but these focus on life cycles in marriage as much as individual development issues (Levenson et al., 1994; Zietlow & Sillars, 1988).

For example, we know that childhood friendships peak in number during adolescence, and adults maintain a few important friendships long-distance. We can document adolescent peer conflicts, but we cannot make strong inferences about how adults experience conflicts with their friends, siblings, or even parents. Nor can we make comparisons regarding how people differentially manage conflicts in their adult relationships, though we suspect they do. The current research conveys an image of many tributaries of relational development leading to one large ocean that we call adulthood, in which there are no particular currents worthy of exploration except within the "Gulf of Marriage."

Hence, the issue of conflict and adulthood development is confounded with information largely obtained from marital contexts. Of course, there are good reasons why psychologists and others have focused on the development of children and the marriages of adults—these transitions and relationships are salient and vitally important. However, whether marital interaction research is really more important than other adult development research is doubtful. Given that past research allows inferences about specific conflict actions in childhood and marriage situations, we can also speculate more on the importance of adult friendships (including adult cross-sex involvements) and adult family relationships (besides marital ones). As the population ages, more of us become interested in knowing where adult incompatibilities arise and how they are managed.

Moreover, as family systems and relationships diversify, researchers may need to expand their conceptualizations and operational definitions of conflict. Developmental progression in single-parent families, relational development and maintenance in long-distance romances and friendships, and commuter involvements all likely entail unique variations of conflict topics and activities. To provide a representative account of conflict in close relationships requires systematic investigation of these modern relationship forms.

Finally, as cultures merge, the likelihood increases for intimate adult intercultural conflicts. Ting-Toomey (1994, in press), for example, observed how U.S. citizens adopt *individualistic* values, whereas some Asian cultures rely on a *collectivistic* orientation. She documented how these two orientations lead to very different understandings, attitudes, and behaviors within intimate conflicts. For example, a person from a collectivist culture would more likely involve close personal friends and family as resources to manage a conflict with a spouse, and that person would see the use of a marital therapist as socially inappropriate. Of course, many individualistic members would rather seek a professional counselor than engage a relative regarding marital problems.

Ting-Toomey (1994, in press) suggested other dimensions for consideration in a multicultural approach to managing close relationship conflicts, beginning with an appreciation for each other's "face" (i.e., one's claimed self-respect). However, Ting-Toomey (1994) concluded, "Of all the dimensions managing intercultural intimate conflict, knowledge is the most critical dimension that underscores the other dimensions of effective intimate conflict management" (p. 66). We hope that future research on conflict in various kinds of adult personal relationships will provide much of this knowledge.

References

Adams, J. (1965). Inequity in social exchange. In L. Berkowitz (Ed.), *Advances in social psychology* (Vol. 2, pp. 267-299). New York: Academic Press.

Alberts, J. K. (1988). An analysis of couples' conversational complaints. *Communication Monographs, 55,* 184-197.

Alberts, J. K. (1989). A descriptive taxonomy of couples' complaint interactions. *Southern Communication Journal, 54,* 125-143.

Alberts, J. K. (1990). Perceived effectiveness of couples' conversational complaints. *Communication Studies, 40,* 280-291.

Alberts, J. K., & Driscoll, G. (1992). Containment versus escalation: The trajectory of couples' conversation complaints. *Western Journal of Communication, 56,* 394-412.

Alexander, J. F. (1973). Defensive and supportive communication in normal and deviant families. *Journal of Consulting and Clinical Psychology, 40,* 223-231.

Amato, P. R., & Keith, B. (1991). Parental divorce and the well-being of children: A meta-analysis. *Psychological Bulletin, 110,* 26-46.

Argyle, M., & Furnham, A. (1983). Sources of satisfaction and conflict in long-term relationships. *Journal of Marriage and the Family, 45,* 481-493.

Attridge, M. (1994). Barriers to dissolution of romantic relationships. In D. J. Canary & L. Stafford (Eds.), *Communication and relational maintenance* (pp. 141-164). San Diego, CA: Academic Press.

Bakeman, R., & Brownlee, J. R. (1982). Social rules governing object conflicts in toddlers and pre-schoolers. In K. H. Rubin & H. S. Ross (Eds.), *Peer relationships and social skills in childhood* (pp. 99-111). New York: Springer-Verlag.

Baucom, D. H., Notarius, C. I., Burnett, C. K., & Haefner, P. (1990). Gender differences and sex-role identity in marriage. In F. D. Fincham & T. Bradbury (Eds.), *The psychology of marriage: Conceptual, empirical, and applied perspectives* (pp. 150-171). New York: Guilford.

Baucom, D. H., Sayers, S. L., & Duhe, A. (1989). Attributional style and attributional patterns among married couples. *Journal of Personality and Social Psychology, 56,* 596-607.

Bavelas, J. B., Rogers, L. E., & Millar, F. E. (1985). Interpersonal conflict. In T. H. Van Dick (Ed.), *Handbook of discourse analysis* (Vol. 4, pp. 9-25). Orlando, FL: Academic Press.

Baxter, L. A. (1979). Self-disclosure as a relationship disengagement strategy: An exploratory investigation. *Human Communication Research, 5,* 215-222.

Baxter, L. A. (1994). A dialogic approach to relationship maintenance. In D. J. Canary & L. Stafford (Eds.), *Communication and relational maintenance* (pp. 233-254). San Diego, CA: Academic Press.

Bell, E. C., & Blakeney, R. N. (1977). Personality correlates of conflict resolution modes. *Human Relations, 30,* 849-857.

Benoit, W. L., & Benoit, P. J. (1988). Factors influencing the accuracy of verbal reports of conversational behavior. *Central States Speech Journal, 39,* 219-232.

Berg, J. H., & McQuinn, R. D. (1986). Attraction and exchange in continuing and noncontinuing dating relationships. *Journal of Personality and Social Psychology, 50,* 942-952.

Berndt, T. J. (1979). Lack of acceptance of reciprocity norms in preschool children. *Developmental Psychology, 15,* 662-663.

Berndt, T. J. (1982). The features and effects of friendships in early adolescence. *Child Development, 53,* 1447-1460.

Berndt, T. J., & Perry, T. B. (1986). Children's perceptions of friendships as supportive relationships. *Developmental Psychology, 22,* 640-648.

Berryman-Fink, C., & Brunner, C. C. (1987). The effects of sex of source and target on interpersonal conflict management styles. *Southern Speech Communication Journal, 53,* 33-48.

Berscheid, E., & Graziano, W. (1979). The initiation of social relationships and interpersonal attraction. In R. L. Burgess & T. L. Huston (Eds.), *Social exchange in developing relationships* (pp. 31-61). New York: Academic Press.

Billings, A. (1979). Conflict resolution in distressed and nondistressed married couples. *Journal of Consulting and Clinical Psychology, 47,* 368-376.

Birchler, G. R., & Webb, L. J. (1977). Discriminating interaction behaviors in happy and unhappy marriages. *Journal of Consulting and Clinical Psychology, 45,* 494-495.

Birchler, G. R., Weiss, R. L., & Vincent, J. P. (1975). Multimethod analysis of social reinforcement exchange between maritally distressed and nondistressed spouse and stranger dyads. *Journal of Personality and Social Psychology, 31,* 349-360.

Blake, R. R., & Mouton, J. S. (1964). *The managerial grid.* Houston, TX: Gulf.

Blake, R. R., & Mouton, J. S. (1970). The fifth achievement. *Journal of Applied Behavioral Science, 6,* 413-426.

Blieszner, R., & Adams, R. G. (1992). *Adult friendship.* Newbury Park, CA: Sage.

Bradbury, T. N., & Fincham, F. D. (1988). Individual difference variables in close relationships: A contextual model of marriage as an integrative framework. *Journal of Personality and Social Psychology, 54,* 713-721.

Bradbury, T. N., & Fincham, F. D. (1990). Attributions in marriage: Review and critique. *Psychological Bulletin, 107,* 3-33.

Braiker, H. B., & Kelley, H. H. (1979). Conflict in the development of close relationships. In R. L. Burgess & T. L. Huston (Eds.), *Social exchange in developing relationships* (pp. 135-168). New York: Academic Press.

Bronfenbrenner, U. (1979). *The ecology of human development: Experiments by nature and design.* Cambridge, MA: Harvard University Press.

Brown, C. T., Yelsma, P., & Keller, P. W. (1981). Communication-conflict predisposition: Development of a theory and an instrument. *Human Relations, 12,* 1103-1117.

Buchanan, C. M., Maccoby, E. E., & Dornbusch, S. M. (1991). Caught between parents: Adolescents' experience in divorced homes. *Child Development, 62,* 1008-1029.

Bukowski, W. M., & Hoza, B. (1989). Popularity and friendship: Issues in theory, measurement, and outcome. In T. J. Berndt & G. W. Ladd (Eds.), *Peer relationships in child development* (pp. 15-45). New York: John Wiley.

Burgess, R. L., & Conger, R. D. (1978). Family interaction in abusive, neglectful, and normal families. *Child Development, 49,* 1163-1173.

Burggraf, C. S., & Sillars, A. L. (1987). A critical examination of sex differences in marital communication. *Communication Monographs, 54,* 276-294.

Burgoon, J. K., & Hale, J. L. (1984). The fundamental topoi of relational communication. *Communication Monographs, 51,* 19-41.

Buhrke, R. A., & Fuqua, D. (1987). Sex differences in same- and cross-sex supportive relationships. *Sex Roles, 17,* 339-352.

Burleson, B. R., & Samter, W. (1994). A social skills approach to relationship maintenance: How individual differences in communication skills affect the achievement of relationship functions. In D. J. Canary & L. Stafford (Eds.), *Communication and relational maintenance* (pp. 61-90). San Diego, CA: Academic Press.

Cahn, D. (Ed.). (1990). *Intimates in conflict: A communication perspective.* Hillsdale, NJ: Lawrence Erlbaum.

Cahn, D. (1992). *Conflict in intimate relationships.* New York: Guilford.

Canary, D. J., Cunningham, E. M., & Cody, M. J. (1988). Goal types, gender, and locus of control in managing interpersonal conflict. *Communication Research, 15,* 426-446.

Canary, D. J., & Cupach, W. R. (1988). Relational and episodic characteristics associated with conflict tactics. *Journal of Social and Personal Relationships, 5,* 305-325.

Canary, D. J., & Hause, K. (1993). Is there any reason to research sex differences in communication? *Communication Quarterly, 41,* 129-144.

Canary, D. J., & Spitzberg, B. H. (1989). A model of perceived competence of conflict strategies. *Human Communication Research, 15,* 630-649.

Canary, D. J., & Spitzberg, B. H. (1990). Attribution biases and associations between conflict strategies and competence outcomes. *Communication Monographs, 57,* 139-151.

Canary, D. J., & Stafford, L. (1992). Relational maintenance strategies and equity in marriage. *Communication Monographs, 59,* 239-267.

Cantor, N., & Khilstrom, J. F. (1987). *Personality and social intelligence.* Englewood Cliffs, NJ: Prentice Hall.

Carver, C. S., & Glass, D. C. (1978). Coronary-prone behavior pattern and interpersonal aggression. *Journal of Personality and Social Psychology, 36,* 361-366.

Christensen, A., & Heavey, C. L. (1990). Gender and social structure in the demand/withdrawal pattern of marital conflict. *Journal of Personality and Social Psychology, 59,* 73-81.

Christensen, A., Sullaway, M., & King, C. (1983). Systematic error in behavioral reports of dyadic interaction: Egocentric bias and content analysis. *Behavioral Therapy, 5,* 129-140.

Claes, M. E. (1992). Friendship and personal adjustment during adolescence. *Journal of Adolescence, 15,* 39-55.

Clark, R. A., & Delia, J. G. (1976). The development of functional persuasive skills in childhood and early adolescence. *Child Development, 47,* 1008-1014.

Cloven, D. H., & Roloff, M. E. (1993). The chilling effect of aggressive potential on the expression of complaints in intimate relationships. *Communication Monographs, 60,* 199-219.

Comstock, J. (1994). Parent-adolescent conflict: A developmental approach. *Western Journal of Communication, 58,* 263-282.

Comstock, J., & Buller, D. B. (1991). Conflict strategies adolescents use with their parents: Testing the cognitive communication characteristics model. *Journal of Language and Social Psychology, 10,* 47-59.

Conrad, C. (1991). Communication in conflict: Style-strategy relationships. *Communication Monographs, 58,* 135-155.

Corsaro, W. A. (1981). Friendship in the nursery school: Social organization in a peer environment. In S. R. Asher & J. M. Gottman (Eds.), *The development of children's friendships* (pp. 207-241). London: Cambridge University Press.

Covey, M. K., & Dengerink, H. A. (1984). Development and validation of a measure of heterosocial conflict resolution ability (Relational Behaviors Survey). *Behavioral Assessment, 6*, 323-332.

Crohan, S. E. (1992). Marital happiness and spousal consensus on beliefs about marital conflict: A longitudinal investigation. *Journal of Social and Personal Relationships, 9*, 89-102.

Cummings, E. M., Iannotti, R. J., & Zahn-Waxler, C. (1985). The influence of conflict between adults on the emotion and aggression of young children. *Developmental Psychology, 21*, 495-507.

Cummings, E. M., Zahn-Waxler, C., & Radke-Yarrow, M. (1984). Developmental changes in children's reactions to anger in the home. *Journal of Child Psychology and Psychiatry, 25*, 63-74.

Cupach, W. R. (1982, May). *Communication satisfaction and interpersonal solidarity as outcomes of conflict message strategy use.* Paper presented at the annual meeting of the International Communication Association Conference, Boston.

Cupach, W. R., & Canary, D. J. (in press). Managing conflict and anger: Investigating the sex stereotype hypothesis. In P. J. Kalbfleisch & M. J. Cody (Eds.), *Gender, power, and communication in human relationships.* Hillsdale, NJ: Lawrence Erlbaum.

Cupach, W. R., & Metts, S. (1994). *Facework.* Thousand Oaks, CA: Sage.

Davitz, J. R. (1969). *The language of emotion.* New York: Academic Press.

Deaux, K., & Lewis, L. L. (1984). The structure of gender stereotypes: Interrelationships among components and gender label. *Journal of Personality and Social Psychology, 46*, 991-1004.

Deaux, K., & Major, B. (1990). A social-psychological model of gender. In D. L. Rhode (Ed.), *Theoretical perspectives on sexual difference* (pp. 89-99). New Haven, CT: Yale University Press.

Delia, J. G., Kline, S. L., & Burleson, B. R. (1979). The development of persuasive communication strategies in kindergartners through twelfth-graders. *Communication Monographs, 46*, 241-256.

Deutsch, M. (1949). A theory of cooperation and competition. *Human Relations, 2*, 129-152.

Deutsch, M. (1973). *The resolution of conflict: Constructive and destructive processes.* New Haven, CT: Yale University Press.

Dindia, K. (1987). The effects of sex of subject and sex of partner on interruptions. *Human Communication Research, 13*, 345-371.

Doherty, W. J. (1981). Cognitive processes in intimate conflict: I. Extending attribution theory. *American Journal of Family Therapy, 9*, 3-13.

Doyle, A. B. (1982). Friends, acquaintances, and strangers: The influence of familiarity and ethnolinguistic background on social interaction. In K. H. Rubin & H. S. Ross (Eds.), *Peer relationships and social skills in childhood* (pp. 229-252). New York: Springer-Verlag.

Duck, S. W., Lock, A., McCall, G., Fitzpatrick, M. A., & Coyne, J. C. (1984). Social and personal relationships: A joint editorial. *Journal of Social and Personal Relationships, 1*, 1-10.

Dunn, J., & Munn, P. (1985). Becoming a family member: Family conflict and the development of social understanding. *Child Development, 56,* 480-492.

Dunn, J., & Munn, P. (1987). Development of justification in disputes with another sibling. *Developmental Psychology, 23,* 791-798.

Dunn, J., & Slomkowski, C. (1992). Conflict and the development of social understanding. In C. U. Shantz & W. W. Hartup (Eds.), *Conflict in child and adolescent development* (pp. 70-92). New York: Cambridge University Press.

Dykstra, P. A. (1990). *Next of (non)kin.* The Netherlands: Swets & Zeitlinger.

Eckerman, C. O., Whatley, J. L., & Kutz, S. L. (1975). Growth of social play with peers during the second year of life. *Developmental Psychology, 11,* 42-49.

Eckerman, C. O., Whatley, J. L., & McGehee, L. J. (1979). Approaching and contacting the object and other manipulates: A social skill of the one-year-old. *Developmental Psychology, 15,* 585-593.

Edwards, J. N., & Brauburger, M. B. (1973). Exchange and parent-youth conflict. *Journal of Marriage and the Family, 35,* 101-106.

Eidelson, R. J., & Epstein, N. (1982). Cognition and relationship maladjustment: Development of a measure of dysfunctional relationship beliefs. *Journal of Consulting and Clinical Psychology, 50,* 715-720.

Eisenberg, A. R. (1992). Conflicts between mothers and their young children. *Merrill-Palmer Quarterly, 38,* 21-43.

Eisenberg, A. R., & Garvey, C. (1981). Children's use of verbal strategies in resolving conflicts. *Discourse Processes, 4,* 149-170.

Emery, R. E. (1982). Interparental conflict and the children of discord and divorce. *Psychological Bulletin, 92,* 310-330.

Emery, R. E. (1992). Family conflicts and their developmental implications: A conceptual analysis of meanings for the structure of relationships. In C. U. Shantz & W. W. Hartup (Eds.), *Conflict in child and adolescent development* (pp. 270-298). New York: Cambridge University Press.

Ericsson, K. A., & Simon, H. A. (1980). Verbal reports as data. *Psychological Review, 87,* 215-251.

Erikson, E. H. (1959). Identity and the life cycle. *Psychological Issues,* Monograph 1. New York: International Universities Press.

Fagot, B. I. (1977). Variations in density: Effect on task and social behaviors of preschool children. *Developmental Psychology, 13,* 166-167.

Fauber, R., Forehand, R., Thomas, A. M., & Wierson, M. (1990). A mediational model of the impact of marital conflict on adolescent adjustment in intact and divorced families: The role of disrupted parenting. *Child Development, 61,* 1112-1123.

Felmlee, D., Sprecher, S., & Bassin, E. (1990). The dissolution of intimate relationships: A hazard model. *Social Psychology Quarterly, 53,* 13-30.

Fiebert, M. S., & Wright, K. S. (1989). Midlife friendships in an American faculty sample. *Psychological Reports, 64,* 1127-1130.

Fincham, F. D., Beach, S. R. H., & Nelson, G. (1987). Attribution processes in distressed and nondistressed couples: 3. Causal and responsibility attributions for spouse behavior. *Cognitive Therapy and Research, 11,* 71-86.

Fincham, F. D., & Bradbury, T. N. (1987a). Cognitive processes and conflict in close relationships: An attribution-efficacy model. *Journal of Personality and Social Psychology, 53,* 1106-1118.

Fincham, F. D., & Bradbury, T. N. (1987b). The impact of attributions in marriage: A longitudinal analysis. *Journal of Personality and Social Psychology, 53,* 510-517.

Fincham, F. D., & Bradbury, T. N. (1992). Assessing attributions in marriage: The relationship attribution measure. *Journal of Personality and Social Psychology, 62,* 457-468.

Fincham, F. D., Bradbury, T. N., & Scott, C. K. (1990). Cognition in marriage. In F. D. Fincham & T. N. Bradbury (Eds.), *The psychology of marriage: Basic issues and applications* (pp. 118-149). New York: Guilford.

Fisher, B. A. (1978). *Perspectives on human communication.* New York: Macmillan.

Fisher, B. A. (1983). Differential effects of sexual composition and interactional context on interaction patterns in dyads. *Human Communication Research, 9,* 225-238.

Fisher, C. B., Reid, J. D., & Melendez, M. (1989). Conflict in families and friendships of later life. *Family Relations, 38,* 83-89.

Fitzpatrick, M. A. (1988a). *Between husbands and wives: Communication in marriage.* Newbury Park, CA: Sage.

Fitzpatrick, M. A. (1988b). Negotiation, problem solving and conflict in various types of marriages. In P. Noller & M. A. Fitzpatrick (Eds.), *Perspectives on marital interaction* (pp. 245-270). Philadelphia, PA: Multilingual Matters.

Fitzpatrick, M. A., Fallis, S., & Vance, L. (1982). Multifunctional coding of conflict resolution strategies in marital dyads. *Family Relations, 31,* 61-70.

Fitzpatrick, M. A., & Winke, T. (1979). You always hurt the one you love: Strategies and tactics in interpersonal conflict. *Communication Quarterly, 27,* 3-11.

Flavell, J. H. (1968). *The development of role-taking and communication skills in children.* New York: John Wiley.

Foster, S. C. (1987). Issues in behavioral assessment of parent-adolescent conflict. *Behavioral Assessment, 9,* 253-269.

Foster, S. L., & Robin, A. L. (1988). Family conflict and communication in adolescence. In E. J. Mash & L. G. Terdal (Eds.), *Behavioral assessment of childhood disorders* (2nd ed., pp. 717-775). New York: Guilford.

Friedman, M., & Rosenman, R. (1974). *Type A behavior and your heart.* New York: Knopf.

Furman, W. (1984). Enhancing children's peer relations and friendships. In S. Duck (Ed.), *Personal relationships 5: Repairing personal relationships* (pp. 103-126). London: Academic Press.

Furman, W. (1987). Acquaintanceship in middle childhood. *Developmental Psychology, 23,* 563-570.

Garvey, C. (1984). *Children's talk.* Cambridge, MA: Harvard University Press.

Gibb, J. R. (1961). Defensive communication. *Journal of Communication, 3,* 141-148.

Goldfried, M. R., & D'Zurilla, T. J. (1969). A behavioral-analytic model for assessing competence. In C. D. Spielberger (Ed.), *Current topics in clinical and community psychology* (Vol. 1, pp. 151-196). New York: Academic Press.

Goodwin, R. (1991). A re-examination of Rusbult's "responses to dissatisfaction" typology. *Journal of Social and Personal Relationships, 8,* 569-574.

Gottman, J. M. (1979). *Marital interaction: Experimental investigations.* New York: Academic Press.

Gottman, J. M. (1982). Emotional responsiveness in marital conversations. *Journal of Communication, 32,* 108-120.

Gottman, J. M. (1983). How children become friends. *Monographs of the Society for Research in Child Development, 48*(2, Serial No. 201).

Gottman, J. M. (1987). The sequential analysis of family interaction. In T. Jacob (Ed.), *Family interaction and psychopathology: Theories, methods, and findings* (pp. 463-478). New York: Plenum.

Gottman, J. M. (1990). Finding the laws of personal relationships. In I. E. Sigel & G. H. Brody (Eds.), *Methods of family research: Biographies of research projects I: Normal families* (pp. 249-263). Hillsdale, NJ: Lawrence Erlbaum.

Gottman, J. M. (1994). *What predicts divorce? The relationship between marital processes and marital outcomes.* Hillsdale, NJ: Lawrence Erlbaum.

Gottman, J. M., & Carrere, S. (1994). Why can't men and women get along? Developmental roots and marital inequities. In D. J. Canary & L. Stafford (Eds.), *Communication and relational maintenance* (pp. 203-229). San Diego, CA: Academic Press.

Gottman, J. M., & Krokoff, L. J. (1989). Marital interaction and marital satisfaction: A longitudinal view. *Journal of Consulting and Clinical Psychology, 57,* 47-52.

Gottman, J. M., & Levenson, R. W. (1988). The social psychophysiology of marriage. In P. Noller & M. A. Fitzpatrick (Eds.), *Perspectives on marital interaction* (pp. 182-200). Philadelphia, PA: Multilingual Matters.

Gottman, J. M., & Levenson, R. W. (1992). Marital processes predictive of later dissolution: Behavior, physiology, and health. *Journal of Personality and Social Psychology, 63,* 221-233.

Gottman, J. M., Markman, H., & Notarius, C. (1977). The topography of marital conflict: A sequential analysis of verbal and nonverbal behavior. *Journal of Marriage and the Family, 39,* 461-477.

Gottman, J. M., & Parkhurst, J. T. (1980). A developmental theory of friendship and acquaintanceship processes. In W. A. Collins (Ed.), *Minnesota symposia on child development: Vol. 13. Development of cognition, affect, and social relations* (pp. 197-253). Hillsdale, NJ: Lawrence Erlbaum.

Hahlweg, K., Reisner, L., Kohli, G., Vollmer, M., Schindler, L., & Revenstorf, D. (1984). Development and validity of a new system to analyze interpersonal communication: Kategoriensystem fur partnerschaftliche Interaktion. In K. Hahlweg & N. S. Jacobson (Eds.), *Marital interaction: Analysis and modification* (pp. 182-197). New York: Guilford.

Hall, J. A. (1987). Parent-adolescent conflict: An empirical review. *Adolescence, 22*, 767-789.

Hammock, G. S., Richardson, D. R., Pilkington, C. J., & Utley, M. (1990). Measurement of conflict in social relationships. *Personality and Individual Differences, 11*, 577-583.

Hartup, W. W. (1974). Aggression in childhood: Developmental perspectives. *American Psychologist, 336-341.*

Hartup, W. W. (1983). Peer relations. In E. M. Hetherington (Ed.), *Handbook of child psychology* (Vol. 4, pp. 103-196). New York: John Wiley.

Hartup, W. W. (1989). Behavioral manifestations of children's friendships. In T. J. Berndt & G. W. Ladd (Eds.), *Peer relationships in child development* (pp. 46-70). New York: John Wiley.

Hartup, W. W. (1992). Conflict and friendship relations. In C. U. Shantz & W. W. Hartup (Eds.), *Conflict in child and adolescent development* (pp. 186-215). New York: Cambridge University Press.

Hartup, W. W., & Laursen, B. (1993). Conflict and context in peer relations. In C. Hart (Ed.), *Children on playgrounds: Research perspectives and applications* (pp. 44-84). Ithaca: State University of New York Press.

Harvey, J. H. (1987). Attributions in close relationships: Recent theoretical developments. *Journal of Social and Clinical Psychology, 5*, 420-434.

Harvey, J. H., Orbuch, T. L., & Weber, A. L. (1990). A social psychological model of account-making in response to severe stress. *Journal of Language and Social Psychology, 9*, 191-207.

Harvey, J. H., Weber, A. L., Galvin, K. S., Hustzi, H. C., & Garnick, N. N. (1986). Attribution and the termination of close relationships. In R. Gilmour & S. Duck (Eds.), *The emerging field of personal relationships* (pp. 189-201). Hillsdale, NJ: Lawrence Erlbaum.

Harvey, J. H., Wells, G. L., & Alvarez, M. D. (1978). Attribution in the context of conflict and separation in close relationships. In J. Harvey, W. Ickes, & R. F. Kidd (Eds.), *New directions in attribution research* (Vol. 2, pp. 235-260). Hillsdale, NJ: Lawrence Erlbaum.

Hatfield, E., Traupmann, J., Sprecher, S., Utne, M., & Hay, M. (1985). Equity in close relationships. In W. Ickes (Ed.), *Compatible and incompatible relationships* (pp. 91-117). New York: Springer-Verlag.

Hatfield, J. D., & Weider-Hatfield, D. (1978). The comparative utility of three types of behavioral units for interaction analysis. *Communication Monographs, 45*, 44-50.

Hay, D. F. (1984). Social conflict in early childhood. In G. Whitehurst (Ed.), *Annals of child development* (Vol. 1, pp. 1-44). Greenwich, CT: JAI.

Hay, D. F., & Ross, H. S. (1982). The social nature of early conflict. *Child Development, 53*, 105-113.

Hays, R. B. (1985). A longitudinal study of friendship development. *Journal of Personality and Social Psychology, 48*, 909-924.

Healey, J. G., & Bell, R. A. (1990). Effects of social networks on individual's responses to conflicts in friendship. In D. D. Cahn (Ed.), *Intimates in conflict: A communication perspective* (pp. 121-152). Hillsdale, NJ: Lawrence Erlbaum.

Hess, R. D., & Camara, K. A. (1979). Post-divorce family relationships as mediating factors in consequences of divorce for children. *Journal of Social Issues, 35*(4), 79-86.

Hinde, R. A. (1976). On describing relationships. *Journal of Child Psychology and Psychiatry, 17*, 1-19.

Hocker, J. L., & Wilmot, W. W. (1991). *Interpersonal conflict* (3rd ed.). Dubuque, IA: William C. Brown.

Holtzworth-Munroe, A., & Jacobson, N. S. (1985). Causal attributions of marital couples: When do they search for causes? What do they conclude when they do? *Journal of Personality and Social Psychology, 48*, 1398-1412.

Holtzworth-Munroe, A., & Jacobson, N. S. (1988). Toward a methodology for coding spontaneous causal attributions: Preliminary results with married couples. *Journal of Social and Clinical Psychology, 7*, 101-112.

Honeycutt, J. M., Woods, B. L., & Fontenot, K. (1993). The endorsement of communication conflict rules as a function of engagement, marriage and marital ideology. *Journal of Social and Personal Relationships, 10*, 285-304.

Horney, K. (1945). *Our inner conflicts: A constructive theory of neurosis.* New York: Norton.

Howes, C. (1983). Patterns of friendship. *Child Development, 54*, 1041-1053.

Hughs, L. A. (1988). "But that's not *really* mean": Competing in a cooperative mode. *Sex Roles, 19*, 669-687.

Infante, D. A. (1987). Aggressiveness. In J. C. McCroskey & J. A. Daly (Eds.), *Personality and interpersonal communication* (pp. 157-192). Newbury Park, CA: Sage.

Infante, D. A., Chandler, T. A., & Rudd, J. E. (1989). Test of an argumentative skill deficiency model of interpersonal violence. *Communication Monographs, 56*, 163-177.

Infante, D. A., & Rancer, A. S. (1982). A conceptualization and measure of argumentativeness. *Journal of Personality Assessment, 46*, 72-80.

Jacob, T. (1974). Patterns of family conflict and dominance as a function of child age and social class. *Developmental Psychology, 10*, 1-12.

Jacobson, N. S. (1985). The role of observational measures in behavior therapy outcome research. *Behavioral Assessment, 7*, 297-308.

James, S. D., & Johnson, D. W. (1987). Social interdependence, psychological adjustment, and marital satisfaction in second marriages. *Journal of Social Psychology, 128*, 287-303.

Jenkins, J. M., & Smith, M. A. (1991). Marital disharmony and children's behavior problems: Aspects of a poor marriage that affect children adversely. *Journal of Child Psychology and Psychiatry and Allied Disciplines, 32*, 793-810.

Jones, E., & Gallois, C. (1989). Spouses' impressions of rules for communication in public and private marital conflicts. *Journal of Marriage and the Family, 51*, 957-967.

Jones, W. H., & Burdette, M. P. (1994). Betrayal in relationships. In A. L. Weber & J. H. Harvey (Eds.), *Perspectives on close relationships* (pp. 243-262). Boston: Allyn & Bacon.

Kabanoff, B. (1987). Predictive validity of the MODE conflict instrument. *Journal of Applied Psychology, 72*, 160-163.

Katz, L. F., Kramer, L., & Gottman, J. M. (1992). Conflict and emotions in marital, sibling, and peer relationships. In C. U. Shantz & W. W. Hartup (Eds.), *Conflict in child and adolescent development* (pp. 122-149). New York: Cambridge University Press.

Kelley, H. H. (1979). *Personal relationships: Their structure and processes.* Hillsdale, NJ: Lawrence Erlbaum.

Kelley, H. H., Cunningham, J. D., Grisham, J. A., Lefebvre, L. M., Sink, C. R., & Yablon, G. (1978). Sex differences in comments made during conflict within close heterosexual pairs. *Sex Roles, 4*, 473-492.

Kelley, H. H., & Thibaut, J. W. (1978). *Interpersonal relations: A theory of interdependence.* New York: John Wiley.

Kelly, C., Huston, T. L., & Cate, R. M. (1985). Premarital relationship correlates of the erosion of satisfaction in marriage. *Journal of Social and Personal Relationships, 2*, 167-178.

Kiecolt-Glaser, J. K., Marlarkey, W. B., Chee, M. A., Newton, T., Cacioppo, J. T., Mao, H. Y., & Glaser, R. (1993). Negative behavior during marital conflict is associated with immunological down-regulation. *Psychosomatic Medicine, 55*, 395-409.

Kilmann, R. H., & Thomas, K. W. (1975). Interpersonal conflict-handling behavior as reflections of Jungian personality dimensions. *Psychological Reports, 37*, 971-980.

Kilmann, R. H., & Thomas, K. W. (1977). Developing a forced-choice measure of conflict-handling behavior: The "MODE" instrument. *Educational and Psychological Measurement, 37*, 309-325.

Knudson, R. M., Sommers, A. A., & Golding, S. L. (1980). Interpersonal perception and mode of resolution in marital conflict. *Journal of Personality and Social Psychology, 38*, 751-763.

Konovsky, M. A., Jaster, F., & McDonald, M. A. (1989). Using parametric statistics to explore the construct validity of the Thomas-Kilmann conflict MODE survey. *Management Communication Quarterly, 3*, 268-290.

Koren, P., Carlton, K., & Shaw, D. (1980). Marital conflict: relations among behaviors, outcomes and distress. *Journal of Consulting and Clinical Psychology, 48*, 460-468.

Krokoff, L. J., Gottman, J. M., & Haas, S. D. (1989). Validation of a rapid couples interaction scoring system. *Behavioral Assessment, 11*, 65-79.

Kuczynski, L., Kochanska, G., Radke-Yarrow, M., & Girnius-Brown, O. (1987). A developmental interpretation of young children's noncompliance. *Developmental Psychology, 23,* 799-806.

La Gaipa, J. J., & Wood, H. D. (1981). Friendship in disturbed adolescents. In S. Duck & R. Gilmour (Eds.), *Personal relationships 3: Personal relationships in disorder* (pp. 169-190). London: Academic Press.

Laursen, B. (1989). *Relationships and conflict during adolescence.* Unpublished doctoral dissertation, University of Minnesota, Minneapolis.

Laursen, B. (1993). The perceived impact of conflict on adolescent relationships. *Merrill-Palmer Quarterly, 39,* 535-550.

Lefcourt, H. M. (1982). *Locus of control: Current trends in theory and research* (2nd ed.). Hillsdale, NJ: Lawrence Erlbaum.

Levenson, R. W., Carstensen, L. L., & Gottman, J. M. (1994). The influence of age and gender on affect, physiology, and their interrelations: A study of long-term marriages. *Journal of Personality and Social Psychology, 67,* 56-68.

Levenson, R. W., & Gottman, J. M. (1983). Marital interaction: Physiological linkage and affective exchange. *Journal of Personality and Social Psychology, 45,* 587-597.

Levenson, R. W., & Gottman, J. M. (1985). Physiological and affective predictors of change in relationship satisfaction. *Journal of Personality and Social Psychology, 49,* 85-94.

Levitt, M. J., Weber, R. A., Clark, M. C., & McDonnell, P. (1985). Reciprocity of exchange in toddler sharing behavior. *Developmental Psychology, 21,* 122-123.

Lewis, M., & Feiring, C. (1981). Direct and indirect interactions in social relationships. *Advances in Infancy Research, 1,* 129-161.

Lewis, R. A., & Spanier, G. B. (1979). Theorizing about the quality and stability of marriage. In W. R. Burr, R. Hill, F. I. Nie, & I. L. Reiss (Eds.), *Contemporary theories about the family* (Vol. 1, pp. 268-294). New York: Free Press.

Lloyd, S. A. (1987). Conflict in premarital relationships: Differential perceptions of males and females. *Family Relations, 36,* 290-294.

Lloyd, S. A. (1990a). A behavioral self-report technique for assessing conflict in close relationships. *Journal of Social and Personal Relationships, 7,* 265-272.

Lloyd, S. A. (1990b). Conflict types and strategies in violent marriages. *Journal of Family Violence, 5,* 269-284.

Lloyd, S. A., & Cate, R. M. (1985). The developmental course of conflict in dissolution of premarital relationships. *Journal of Social and Personal Relationships, 2,* 179-194.

Lloyd, S. A., & Emery, B. C. (1994). Physically aggressive conflict in romantic relationships. In D. D. Cahn (Ed.), *Conflict in personal relationships* (pp. 27-46). Hillsdale, NJ: Lawrence Erlbaum.

Lytton, H. (1979). Disciplinary encounter between young boys and their mothers and fathers: Is there a contingency system? *Developmental Psychology, 15,* 256-268.

MacCombie, D. J. (1978). *The development of reciprocity in children's social interchanges.* Unpublished doctoral dissertation, University of North Carolina, Chapel Hill.

Margolin, G. (1990). Marital conflict. In G. H. Brody & I. E. Siegel (Eds.), *Methods of family research: Biographies of research projects. Vol. II. Clinical populations* (pp. 191-225). Hillsdale, NJ: Lawrence Erlbaum.

Margolin, G., Burman, B., & John, R. S. (1989). Home observations of married couples reenacting naturalistic conflicts. *Behavioral Assessment, 11,* 101-118.

Margolin, G., & Wampold, B. E. (1981). Sequential analysis of conflict and accord in distressed and nondistressed marital partners. *Journal of Consulting and Clinical Psychology, 49,* 554-567.

Markman, H. J. (1979). Application of a behavioral model of marriage in predicting relationship satisfaction of couples planning marriage. *Journal of Consulting and Clinical Psychology, 47,* 743-749.

Markman, H. J. (1981). Prediction of marital distress: A 5-year follow-up. *Journal of Consulting and Clinical Psychology, 49,* 760-762.

Markman, H. J., & Notarius, C. L. (1987). Coding marital and family interaction: Current status. In T. Jacob (Ed.), *Family interaction and psychopathology: Theories, methods, and findings* (pp. 329-390). New York: Plenum.

Marlarkey, W. B., Kiecolt-Glaser, J. K., Perl, D., & Glaser, R. (1994). Hostile behavior during marital conflict alters pituitary and adrenal hormones. *Psychosomatic Medicine, 56,* 41-51.

Marshall, L. L. (1994). Physical and psychological abuse. In W. R. Cupach & B. H. Spitzberg (Eds.), *The dark side of interpersonal communication* (pp. 281-311). Hillsdale, NJ: Lawrence Erlbaum.

Matthews, K. A. (1982). Psychological perspectives on the Type A behavior pattern. *Psychological Bulletin, 91,* 293-323.

Matthews, S. H. (1986). *Friendships through the life course: Oral biographies in old age.* Beverly Hills, CA: Sage.

Maynard, D. W. (1985). How children start arguments. *Language in Society, 14,* 207-223.

McGonagle, K. A., Kessler, R. C., & Gotlib, I. H. (1993). The effects of marital disagreement style, frequency, and outcome on marital disruption. *Journal of Social and Personal Relationships, 10,* 385-404.

McGonagle, K. A., Kessler, R. C., & Schilling, E. A. (1992). The frequency and determinants of marital disagreements in a community sample. *Journal of Social and Personal Relationships, 9,* 507-524.

Mead, D. E., Vatcher, G. M., Wyne, B. A., & Roberts, S. L. (1990). The comprehensive areas of change questionnaire: Assessing marital couples' presenting complaints. *American Journal of Family Therapy, 18,* 65-79.

Mead, G. H. (1934). *Mind, self, and society.* Chicago: University of Chicago Press.

Messman, S. J., & Mikesell, R. L. (1994, April). *An exploratory investigation of competition in close relationships.* Paper presented at the annual meeting of the Eastern Communication Association, Washington, DC.

Metts, S. (1994). Relational transgressions. In W. R. Cupach & B. H. Spitzberg (Eds.), *The dark side of interpersonal communication* (pp. 217-239). Hillsdale, NJ: Lawrence Erlbaum.

Metts, S., & Cupach, W. R. (1990). The influence of relationship beliefs and problem-solving responses on satisfaction in romantic relationships. *Human Communication Research, 17,* 170-185.

Metts, S., & Cupach, W. R. (1993, June). *Factors influencing closeness in opposite-sex relationships.* Paper presented at the Fourth International Conference of Personal Relationships, Milwaukee, WI.

Metts, S., Sprecher, S., & Cupach, W. R. (1991). Retrospective self-reports. In B. Montgomery & S. Duck (Eds.), *Studying interpersonal interaction* (pp. 162-178). New York: Guilford.

Miller, P. C., Lefcourt, H. M., Holmes, J. G., Ware, E. E., & Saleh, W. E. (1986). Marital locus of control and marital problem-solving. *Journal of Personality and Social Psychology, 51,* 161-169.

Minuchin, P. (1992). Conflict and child maltreatment. In C. U. Shantz & W. W. Hartup (Eds.), *Conflict in child and adolescent development* (pp. 380-401). New York: Cambridge University Press.

Montemayor, R. (1983). Parents and adolescents in conflict. All forms some of the time and some forms most of the time. *Journal of Early Adolescence, 3,* 83-103.

Montemayor, R. (1986). Family variation in parent-adolescent storm and stress. *Journal of Adolescent Research, 1,* 15-31.

Nadelman, L., & Begun, A. (1982). The effect of the newborn on the older sibling: Mother's questionnaires. In M. E. Lamb & B. Sutton-Smith (Eds.), *Sibling relationships: Their nature and significance across the lifespan* (pp. 83-115). Hillsdale, NJ: Lawrence Erlbaum.

Napier, A. Y. (1978). The rejection-intrusion pattern: A central family dynamic. *Journal of Marriage and Family Counseling, 4,* 5-12.

Newton, D. A., & Burgoon, J. K. (1990a). Nonverbal conflict behaviors: Functions, strategies, and tactics. In D. D. Cahn (Ed.), *Intimates in conflict: A communication perspective* (pp. 77-104). Hillsdale, NJ: Lawrence Erlbaum.

Newton, D. A., & Burgoon, J. K. (1990b). The use and consequences of verbal influence strategies during interpersonal disagreements. *Human Communication Research, 16,* 477-518.

Noller, P., Feeney, J. A., Bonnell, D., & Callan, V. J. (1994). A longitudinal study of conflict in early marriage. *Journal of Social and Personal Relationships, 11,* 233-252.

Notarius, C. I., Markman, H. J., & Gottman, J. M. (1983). Couples interaction scoring system: Clinical application. In E. E. Filsinger (Ed.), *Marriage and family assessment* (pp. 117-151). Beverly Hills, CA: Sage.

O'Keefe, B. J., & Benoit, P. J. (1982). Children's arguments. In J. R. Cox & C. A. Willard (Eds.), *Advances in argumentation theory and research* (pp. 154-183). Carbondale: Southern Illinois University Press.

Olson, D. H., & Ryder, R. G. (1970). Inventory of marital conflicts (IMC): An experimental interaction procedure. *Journal of Marriage and the Family, 32,* 443-448.

Orvis, B. R., Kelley, H. H., & Butler, D. (1976). Attributional conflict in young couples. In J. H. Harvey, W. J. Ickes, & R. Kidd (Eds.), *New directions in attribution research* (Vol. 1, pp. 353-386). Hillsdale, NJ: Lawrence Erlbaum.

Osborne, L. N., & Fincham, F. D. (1994). Conflict between parents and their children. In D. D. Cahn (Ed.), *Conflict in personal relationships* (pp. 117-141). Hillsdale, NJ: Lawrence Erlbaum.

Paikoff, R. L., & Brooks-Gunn, J. (1991). Do parent-child relationships change during puberty? *Psychological Bulletin, 110,* 47-66.

Parke, R. D. (1979). Interactional designs. In R. B. Cairns (Ed.), *The analysis of social interactions methods, issues, and illustrations* (pp. 15-35). Hillsdale, NJ: Lawrence Erlbaum.

Parker, J. G., & Gottman, J. M. (1989). Social and emotional development in a relational context: Friendship interaction from early childhood to adolescence. In T. J. Berndt & G. W. Ladd (Eds.), *Peer relationships in child development* (pp. 95-132). New York: John Wiley.

Parks, M. (1982). Ideology in interpersonal communication: Off the couch and into the world. In M. Burgoon (Ed.), *Communication yearbook 6* (pp. 79-107). Beverly Hills, CA: Sage.

Patterson, G. R. (1979). A performance theory for coercive family interaction. In R. B. Cairns (Ed.), *The analysis of social interactions* (pp. 119-162). Hillsdale, NJ: Lawrence Erlbaum.

Patterson, G. R. (1982). *Coercive family processes.* Eugene, OR: Castalia.

Peck, K. (1988). When the family is not a household word: Alternative living arrangements. *The Progressive, 52*(9), 16-17.

Perlman, D., & Fehr, B. (1987). The development of intimate relationships. In D. Perlman & S. Duck (Eds.), *Intimate relationships: Dynamics, development, and deterioration* (pp. 13-42). Newbury Park, CA: Sage.

Peterson, D. R. (1983). Conflict. In H. H. Kelley, E. Berscheid, A. Christensen, J. H. Harvey, T. L. Huston, G. Levinger, E. McClintock, L. A. Peplau, & D. R. Peterson (Eds.), *Close relationships* (pp. 360-396). New York: Freeman.

Piaget, J. (1932). *The moral judgement and reasoning in the child.* London: Routledge & Kegan Paul.

Pike, G. R., & Sillars, A. L. (1985). Reciprocity of marital communication. *Journal of Social and Personal Relationships, 2,* 303-324.

Pistole, M. C. (1989). Attachment in adult romantic relationships: Styles of conflict resolution and relationship satisfaction. *Journal of Social and Personal Relationships, 6,* 505-510.

Ponzetti, J. J. Jr., & Cate, R. M. (1987). The developmental course of conflict in the marital dissolution process. *Journal of Divorce, 10,* 1-15.

Prinz, R. J. (1976). *The assessment of parent-adolescent relations: Discriminating distressed and nondistressed dyads.* Unpublished doctoral dissertation, State University of New York, Stony Brook.

Prinz, R. J., Foster, S. L., Kent, R. N., & O'Leary, K. D. (1979). Multivariate assessment of conflict in distressed and nondistressed mother-adolescent dyads. *Journal of Applied Behavior Analysis, 12,* 691-700.

Prinz, R. J., & Kent, R. N. (1978). Recording parent-adolescent interactions without the use of frequency or interval-by-interval coding. *Behavior Therapy, 9,* 602-604.

Prinz, R. J., Rosenblum, R. S., & O'Leary, K. D. (1978). Affective communication differences between distressed and nondistressed mother-adolescent dyads. *Journal of Abnormal Child Psychology, 6,* 373-383.

Putnam, L. L. (1988). Communication and interpersonal conflict in organizations. *Management Communication Quarterly, 1,* 293-301.

Putnam, L. L., & Wilson, C. E. (1982). Communicative strategies in organizational conflicts: Reliability and validity of a measurement scale. In M. Burgoon (Ed.), *Communication yearbook 6* (pp. 629-652). Beverly Hills, CA: Sage.

Ragan, S. L. (1989). Communication between the sexes: A consideration of differences in adult communication. In J. F. Nussbaum (Ed.), *Life-span communication: Normative processes* (pp. 179-193). Hillsdale, NJ: Lawrence Erlbaum.

Rahim, M. A. (1983). A measure of styles of handling interpersonal conflict. *Academy of Management Journal, 26,* 368-376.

Rands, M., Levinger, G., & Mellinger, G. D. (1981). Patterns of conflict resolution and marital satisfaction. *Journal of Family Issues, 2,* 297-321.

Raush, H. L., Barry, W. A., Hertel, R. J., & Swain, M. A. (1974). *Communication, conflict, and marriage.* San Francisco: Jossey-Bass.

Rawlins, W. K. (1992). *Friendship matters: Communication, dialectics, and the life course.* Hawthorne, NY: Aldine.

Rawlins, W. K. (1994). Being there and growing apart: Sustaining friendships during adulthood. In D. J. Canary & L. Stafford (Eds.), *Communication and relational maintenance* (pp. 275-296). San Diego, CA: Academic Press.

Renshaw, P., & Asher, S. R. (1983). Children's goals and strategies for social interaction. *Merrill-Palmer Quarterly, 29,* 353-374.

Resick, P. A., Barr, P. K., Sweet, J. J., Kieffer, D. M., Ruby, N. L., & Spiegel, D. K. (1981). Perceived and actual discriminators of conflict from accord in marital communication. *American Journal of Family Therapy, 9*(1), 58-68.

Revenstorf, D., Hahlweg, K., Schindler, L., & Vogel, B. (1984). Interaction analysis of marital conflict. In K. Hahlweg & N. S. Jacobson (Eds.), *Marital interaction: Analysis and modification* (pp. 159-181). New York: Guilford.

Rizzo, R. A. (1989). *Friendship development among children in school.* Norwood, NJ: Ablex.

Robin, A. L., & Foster, S. L. (1989). *Negotiating parent-adolescent conflict: A behavioral systems approach.* New York: Guilford.

Roloff, M. E. (1976). Communication strategies, relationships, and relational change. In G. R. Miller (Ed.), *Explorations in interpersonal communication* (pp. 173-195). Beverly Hills, CA: Sage.

Roloff, M. E. (1981). *Interpersonal communication: The social exchange approach.* Beverly Hills, CA: Sage.

Roloff, M. E. (1987). Communication and conflict. In C. R. Berger & S. H. Chaffee (Eds.), *Handbook of communication science* (pp. 484-534). Newbury Park, CA: Sage.

Roloff, M. E., & Cloven, D. H. (1990). The chilling effect in interpersonal relationships: The reluctance to speak one's mind. In D. D. Cahn (Ed.), *Intimates in conflict: A communication perspective* (pp. 49-76). Hillsdale, NJ: Lawrence Erlbaum.

Roloff, M. E., & Cloven, D. H. (1994). When partners transgress: Maintaining violated relationships. In D. J. Canary & L. Stafford (Eds.), *Communication and relational maintenance* (pp. 23-43). San Diego, CA: Academic Press.

Rose, S. M. (1985). Same- and cross-sex friendships and the psychology of homosociality. *Sex Roles, 12*, 63-74.

Rosenberger, L. M., & Strube, M. J. (1986). The influence of Type A and B behavior patterns on the perceived quality of dating relationships. *Journal of Applied Social Psychology, 16*, 277-286.

Rosenthal, D. A., Demetriou, A., & Efklides, A. (1989). A cross-national study of the influence of culture on conflict between parents and adolescents. *International Journal of Behavioral Development, 12*, 207-220.

Ross, R. G., & DeWine, S. (1988). Assessing the Ross-DeWine conflict management message style (CMMS). *Management Communication Quarterly, 1*, 414-429.

Rusbult, C. E. (1987). Responses to dissatisfaction in close relationships: The exit-voice-loyalty-neglect model. In D. Perlman & S. Duck (Eds.), *Intimate relationships: Development, dynamics, and deterioration* (pp. 209-237). Newbury Park, CA: Sage.

Rusbult, C. E. (1993). Understanding responses to dissatisfaction in close relationships. The exit-voice-loyalty-neglect model. In S. Worchel & J. A. Simpson (Eds.), *Conflict between people and groups: Causes, processes, and resolutions* (pp. 30-59). Chicago: Nelson-Hall.

Rusbult, C. E., Johnson, D. J., & Morrow, G. D. (1986a). Determinants and consequences of exit, voice, loyalty, and neglect: Responses to dissatisfaction in adult romantic involvements. *Human Relations, 39*, 45-63.

Rusbult, C. E., Johnson, D. J., & Morrow, G. D. (1986b). Impact of couple patterns of problem solving on distress and nondistress in dating relationships. *Journal of Personality and Social Psychology, 50*, 744-753.

Rusbult, C. E., Verette, J., Whitney, G. A., Slovik, L. F., & Lipkus, I. (1991). Accommodation processes in close relationships: Theory and preliminary empirical evidence. *Journal of Personality and Social Psychology, 60,* 53-78.

Rusbult, C. E., & Zembrodt, I. M. (1983). Responses to dissatisfaction in romantic involvements: A multidimensional scaling analysis. *Journal of Experimental Social Psychology, 19,* 274-293.

Rusbult, C. E., Zembrodt, I. M., & Gunn, L. K. (1982). Exit, voice, loyalty, and neglect: Responses to dissatisfaction in romantic involvements. *Journal of Personality and Social Psychology, 43,* 1230-1242.

Schaap, C. (1982). *Communication and adjustment in marriage.* The Netherlands: Swets & Zeitlinger.

Schaap, C. (1984). A comparison of the interaction of distressed and non-distressed married couples in a laboratory situation: Literature survey, methodological issues, and an empirical investigation. In K. Hahlweg & N. S. Jacobson (Eds.), *Marital interaction: Analysis and modification* (pp. 133-158). New York: Guilford.

Schaap, C., Buunk, B., & Kerkstra, A. (1988). Marital conflict resolution. In P. Noller & M. A. Fitzpatrick (Eds.), *Perspectives on marital interaction* (pp. 203-244). Philadelphia, PA: Multilingual Matters.

Selman, R. L. (1980). *The growth of interpersonal understanding: Developmental and clinical analyses.* New York: Academic Press.

Selman, R. L. (1981). The child as a friendship philosopher. In S. R. Asher & J. M. Gottman (Eds.), *The development of children's friendships* (pp. 242-272). London: Cambridge University Press.

Shantz, C. U. (1987). Conflicts between children. *Child Development, 58,* 283-305.

Shantz, C. U. (1993). Children's conflicts: Representations and lessons learned. In R. R. Cocking & K. A. Renninger (Eds.), *The development and meaning of psychological distance* (pp. 185-202). Hillsdale, NJ: Lawrence Erlbaum.

Shantz, C. U., & Hartup, W. W. (1992). Conflict and development: An introduction. In C. U. Shantz & W. W. Hartup (Eds.), *Conflict in child and adolescent development* (pp. 1-11). New York: Cambridge University Press.

Shantz, C. U., & Hobart, C. J. (1989). Social conflict and development: Peers and siblings. In T. J. Berndt & G. W. Ladd (Eds.), *Peer relationships in child development* (pp. 71-94). New York: John Wiley.

Shantz, D. W. (1986). Conflict, aggression, and peer status: An observational study. *Child Development, 57,* 1322-1332.

Sharabany, R., Gershoni, R., & Hofman, J. E. (1981). Girlfriend, boyfriend: Age and sex differences in intimate friendships. *Developmental Psychology, 17,* 800-808.

Shimanoff, S. (1980). *Communication rules: Theory and research.* Beverly Hills, CA: Sage.

Sillars, A. L. (1980a). Attributions and communication in roommate conflicts. *Communication Monographs, 47,* 180-200.

Sillars, A. L. (1980b). The sequential and distributional structure of conflict interactions as a function of attributions concerning the locus of responsibility and stability of conflicts. In D. Nimmo (Ed.), *Communication yearbook 4* (pp. 217-235). New Brunswick, NJ: Transaction Publishing.

Sillars, A. L. (1981). Attributions and interpersonal conflict resolution. In J. H. Harvey, W. Ickes, & R. Kidd (Eds.), *New directions in attribution research* (Vol. 3, pp. 281-306). Hillsdale, NJ: Lawrence Erlbaum.

Sillars, A. L. (1985). Interpersonal perception in relationships. In W. Ickes (Ed.), *Compatible and incompatible relationships* (pp. 277-305). New York: Springer-Verlag.

Sillars, A. L. (1986, April). *Procedures for coding interpersonal conflict (revised)* (Manual). Missoula: University of Montana, Department of Interpersonal Communication.

Sillars, A. L., Coletti, S. F., Parry, D., & Rogers, M. A. (1982). Coding verbal conflicts: Non-verbal and perceptual correlates of the "avoidance-distributive-integrative" distinction. *Human Communication Research, 9,* 83-95.

Sillars, A. L., Pike, G. R., Jones, T. S., & Murphy, M. A. (1984). Communication and understanding in marriage. *Human Communication Research, 10,* 317-350.

Sillars, A. L., Pike, G. R., Jones, T. S., & Redmon, K. (1983). Communication and conflict in marriage. In R. N. Bostrom (Ed.), *Communication yearbook 7* (pp. 414-429). Beverly Hills, CA: Sage.

Sillars, A. L., & Scott, M. D. (1983). Interpersonal perception between intimates: An integrative review. *Human Communication Research, 10,* 153-176.

Sillars, A. L., & Weisberg, J. (1987). Conflict as a social skill. In M. E. Roloff & G. R. Miller (Eds.), *Interpersonal processes: New directions in communication research* (pp. 140-171). Newbury Park, CA: Sage.

Sillars, A. L., Weisberg, J., Burggraf, C. S., & Zietlow, P. H. (1990). Communication and understanding revisited: Married couples' understanding and recall of conversations. *Communication Research, 17,* 500-522.

Sillars, A. L., & Wilmot, W. W. (1989). Marital communication across the life span. In J. F. Nussbaum (Ed.), *Life-span communication: Normative processes* (pp. 225-253). Hillsdale, NJ: Lawrence Erlbaum.

Sillars, A. L., & Wilmot, W. W. (1994). Communication strategies in conflict and mediation. In J. A. Daly & J. M. Wiemann (Eds.), *Strategic interpersonal communication* (pp. 163-190). Hillsdale, NJ: Lawrence Erlbaum.

Smetana, J. G. (1988). Adolescents' and parents' conceptions of parental authority. *Child Development, 59,* 321-335.

Smetana, J. G. (1989). Adolescents' and parents' reasoning about actual family conflict. *Child Development, 60,* 1052-1067.

Smetana, J. G., Braeges, J. L., & Yau, J. (1991). Doing what you say and saying what you do: Reasoning about adolescent-parent conflict. *Journal of Adolescent Research, 6,* 276-295.

Smetana, J., Yau, J., Restropo, A., & Braeges, J. L. (1991). Adolescent-parent conflict in married and divorced families. *Developmental Psychology, 27,* 1000-1010.

Smith, D. E. (1993). The standard North American family. *Journal of Family Issues, 14*, 50-65.

Smollar, J., & Youniss, J. (1982). Social development through friendship. In K. H. Rubin & H. S. Ross (Eds.), *Peer relationships and social skills in children* (pp. 270-298). New York: Springer-Verlag.

Spitzberg, B. H., Canary, D. J., & Cupach, W. R. (1994). A competence-based approach to the study of interpersonal conflict. In D. D. Cahn (Ed.), *Conflict in personal relationships* (pp. 183-202). Hillsdale, NJ: Lawrence Erlbaum.

Sprecher, S., & Felmlee, D. (1993). Conflict, love and other relationship dimensions for individuals in dissolving, stable, and growing premarital relationships. *Free Inquiry in Creative Sociology, 21*(2), 1-12.

Sprey, J. (1971). On the management of conflict in families. *Journal of Marriage and the Family, 33*, 722-731.

Stafford, L., & Bayer, C. C. (1993). *Interaction between parents and children.* Newbury Park, CA: Sage.

Stafford, L., & Canary, D. J. (1991). Maintenance strategies and romantic relationship type, gender, and relational characteristics. *Journal of Social and Personal Relationships, 8*, 217-242.

Steinberg, L. (1981). Transformations in family relations at puberty. *Developmental Psychology, 17*, 833-840.

Steinberg, L. D. (1987). The impact of puberty on family relations: Effects of pubertal status and pubertal timing. *Developmental Psychology, 25*, 451-460.

Steinberg, L. D., & Hill, J. P. (1978). Patterns of family interaction as a function of age, the onset of puberty, and formal thinking. *Developmental Psychology, 14*, 683-684.

Sternberg, R. J., & Dobson, D. M. (1987). Resolving interpersonal conflicts: An analysis of stylistic consistency. *Journal of Personality and Social Psychology, 52*, 794-812.

Sternberg, R. J., & Soriano, L. J. (1984). Styles of conflict resolution. *Journal of Personality and Social Psychology, 47*, 115-126.

Stillwell, R., & Dunn, J. (1985). Continuities in sibling relationships: Patterns of aggression and friendliness. *Journal of Child Psychology and Psychiatry, 26*, 627-637.

Stocker, C. M. (1989). *Sibling relationships in childhood: Links with friendships and peer relationships.* Unpublished doctoral dissertation, Pennsylvania State University, University Park.

Storms, M. D. (1973). Videotape and the attribution process: Reversing actors' and observers' points of view. *Journal of Personality and Social Psychology, 27*, 165-175.

Straus, M. A. (1979). Measuring intrafamily conflict and violence: The conflict tactics (CT) scales. *Journal of Marriage and the Family, 41*, 75-88.

Strawbridge, W. J., & Wallhagen, M. I. (1991). Impact of family conflict on adult caregivers. *The Gerontologist, 31*(6), 770-777.

Strodbeck, F. L. (1951). Husband-wife interaction over revealed differences. *American Sociological Review, 16*, 468-473.

Sullivan, H. S. (1953). *The interpersonal theory of psychology.* New York: Norton.

Tannen, D. (1990). *You just don't understand: Women and men in conversation.* New York: William Morrow.

Thomas, K. W., & Pondy, L. R. (1977). Toward an "intent" model of conflict management among principal parties. *Human Relations, 30*, 1089-1102.

Ting-Toomey, S. (1983a). An analysis of verbal communication patterns in high and low marital adjustment groups. *Human Communication Research, 9*, 306-319.

Ting-Toomey, S. (1983b). Coding conversation between intimates: A validation study of the intimate negotiation coding system (INCS). *Communication Quarterly, 31*, 68-77.

Ting-Toomey, S. (1994). Managing conflict in intimate intercultural relationships. In D. D. Cahn (Ed.), *Conflict in personal relationships* (pp. 47-77). Hillsdale, NJ: Lawrence Erlbaum.

Ting-Toomey, S. (in press). Conflict in intercultural contexts. In W. R. Cupach & D. J. Canary (Eds.), *Competence in interpersonal conflict.* New York: McGraw-Hill.

Utley, M. E., Richardson, D. R., & Pilkington, C. J. (1989). Personality and interpersonal conflict management. *Personality and Individual Differences, 10*, 287-293.

Valsiner, J., & Cairns, R. B. (1992). Theoretical perspectives on conflict and development. In C. U Shantz & W. W. Hartup (Eds.), *Conflict in child and adolescent development* (pp. 15-35). New York: Cambridge University Press.

Vander Zanden, J. W. (1980). *Human development* (2nd ed.). New York: Knopf.

van de Vliert, E., & Euwema, M. C. (1994). Agreeableness and activeness as components of conflict behaviors. *Journal of Personality and Social Psychology, 66*, 674-687.

Van Egeren, L. F. (1979). Social interactions, communications, and the coronary-prone behavior pattern: A psychophysiological study. *Psychosomatic Medicine, 41*, 2-18.

Van Yperen, N. W., & Buunk, B. (1990). A longitudinal study of equity and satisfaction in intimate relationships. *European Journal of Social Psychology, 20*, 287-309.

Vaughn, B. E., Kopp, C. B., & Krakow, J. B. (1984). The emergence and consolidation of self-control from eighteen to thirty months of age: Normative trends and individual differences. *Child Development, 55*, 990-1004.

Vincent, J. P., Weiss, R. L., & Birchler, G. R. (1975). A behavioral analysis of problem-solving in married and stranger dyads. *Behavior Therapy, 6*, 475-487.

Vuchinich, S. (1984). Sequencing and social structure in family conflict. *Social Psychology Quarterly, 47,* 217-234.

Vuchinich, S. (1987). Starting and stopping spontaneous family conflicts. *Journal of Marriage and the Family, 49,* 591-601.

Vuchinich, S. (1990). The sequential organization of closing in verbal family conflict. In A. D. Grimshaw (Ed.), *Conflict talk: Sociolinguistic investigations of arguments in conversations* (pp. 118-138). New York: Cambridge University Press.

Vuchinich, S., Emery, R. E., & Cassidy, J. (1988). Family members as third parties in dyadic family conflict: Strategies, alliances, and outcomes. *Child Development, 59,* 1293-1302.

Watzlawick, P., Beavin, J., & Jackson, D. D. (1967). *Pragmatics of human communication: A study of interactional patterns, pathologies, and paradoxes.* New York: Norton.

Weber, A. L., Harvey, J. H., & Orbuch, T. L. (1992). What went wrong: Communicating accounts of relationship conflict. In M. L. McLaughlin, M. J. Cody, & S. J. Read (Eds.), *Explaining one's self to others: Reason-giving in a social context* (pp. 261-280). Hillsdale, NJ: Lawrence Erlbaum.

Weider-Hatfield, D. (1988). Assessing the Rahim organizational conflict inventory–II (ROCI–II). *Management Communication Quarterly, 1,* 350-366.

Weider-Hatfield, D. (1993, November). *The role of communication in conflict: Revisiting communication scholars' assumptions about the nature of conflict.* Paper presented at the annual meeting of the Speech Communication Association, Miami, FL.

Weiss, R. L. (1984). Cognitive and behavioral measures of marital interaction. In K. Hahlweg & N. S. Jacobson (Eds.), *Marital interaction: Analysis and modification* (pp. 232-252). New York: Guilford.

Weiss, R. L. (1993). *Marital Interaction Coding System–IV (MICS–IV).* Unpublished coding manual, University of Oregon, Eugene.

Weiss, R. L., & Dehle, C. (1994). Cognitive behavioral perspectives on marital conflict. In D. D. Cahn (Ed.), *Conflict in personal relationships* (pp. 95-115). Hillsdale, NJ: Lawrence Erlbaum.

Weiss, R. L., Hops, H., & Patterson, G. R. (1973). A framework for conceptualizing marital conflict: A technology for altering it, some data for evaluating it. In F. W. Clark & L. A. Hamerlynck (Eds.), *Critical issues in research and practice: Proceedings of the Fourth Banff International Conference on Behavior Modification* (pp. 309-342). Champaign, IL: Research Press.

Weiss, R. L., & Summers, K. J. (1983). Marital interaction coding system–III. In E. E. Filsinger (Ed.), *Marriage and family assessment: A sourcebook for family therapy* (pp. 85-115). Beverly Hills, CA: Sage.

Weiss, R. S. (1986). Continuities and transformations in social relationships from childhood to adulthood. In W. W. Hartup & Z. Rubin (Eds.), *Relationships and development* (pp. 95-110). Hillsdale, NJ: Lawrence Erlbaum.

Whittaker, S., & Bry, B. H. (1991). Overt and covert parental conflict and adolescent problems: Observed marital interaction in clinic and nonclinic families. *Adolescence, 26,* 865-876.

Wilkins, B. M., & Andersen, P. A. (1991). Gender differences and similarities in management communication: A meta-analysis. *Management Communication Quarterly, 5,* 6-35.

Williamson, R. N., & Fitzpatrick, M. A. (1985). Two approaches to marital interaction: Relational control patterns in marital types. *Communication Monographs, 52,* 236-252.

Wilmot, W. W. (1987). *Dyadic communication* (2nd ed.). New York: Random House.

Wiseman, J. P. (1986). Friendship: Bonds and binds in a voluntary relationship. *Journal of Social and Personal Relationships, 3,* 191-211.

Witteman, H. (1988). Interpersonal problem solving: Problem conceptualization and communication use. *Communication Monographs, 55,* 336-359.

Witteman, H. (1992). Analyzing interpersonal conflict: Nature of awareness, type of initiating event, situational perceptions, and management styles. *Western Journal of Communication, 56,* 248-280.

Witteman, H., & Fitzpatrick, M. A. (1986). Compliance-gaining in marital interaction: Power bases, processes, and outcomes. *Communication Monographs, 53,* 130-143.

Womack, D. F. (1988). Assessing the Thomas-Kilmann conflict MODE survey. *Management Communication Quarterly, 1,* 321-349.

Yelsma, P. (1981). Conflict predispositions: Differences between happy and clinical couples. *American Journal of Family Therapy, 9,* 57-63.

Youniss, J. (1980). *Parents and peers in social development.* Chicago: University of Chicago Press.

Youniss, J., & Volpe, J. (1978). A relational analysis of children's friendship. In W. Damon (Ed.), *Social cognition: New directions for child development* (pp. 1-22). San Francisco: Jossey-Bass.

Zietlow, P. H., & Sillars, A. L. (1988). Life-stage differences in communication during marital conflicts. *Journal of Social and Personal Relationships, 5,* 223-245.

Zillman, D. (1990). The interplay of cognition and excitation in aggravated conflict. In D. D. Cahn (Ed.), *Intimates in conflict: A communication perspective* (pp. 187-208). Hillsdale, NJ: Lawrence Erlbaum.

Index

About the Authors

Daniel J. Canary is Professor of Speech Communication at Pennsylvania State University, University Park, Pennsylvania. He received his doctorate in Communication Arts and Sciences from the University of Southern California in 1983. His research explores conflict management and argument, relationship maintenance activities, and sex differences/similarities. He is coauthor (with Michael Cody) of *Interpersonal Communication: A Goals-Based Approach* and coeditor (with Laura Stafford) of *Communication and Relational Maintenance.* He is the author or coauthor of numerous articles and book chapters, as well as an editorial board member of several communication journals.

William R. Cupach is Professor of Communication at Illinois State University, Normal, Illinois. He received his doctorate in Communication Arts and Sciences from the University of Southern California in 1981. He is coauthor (with Sandra Metts) of *Facework,* which is also in the Sage Series on Close Relationships. With Brian Spitzberg, he coedited *The Dark Side of Interpersonal Communication* and coauthored *Interpersonal Communication Competence* and *Handbook of Interpersonal Competence.* His research focuses on the management of problematic, awkward, and challenging episodes in personal relationships. Currently, he serves as an Associate Editor for Communication of the *Journal of Social and Personal Relationships.*

Susan J. Messman is Lecturer of Speech Communication at Pennsylvania State University, University Park, Pennsylvania. She earned her doctorate in Interpersonal Communication from Ohio University in 1995. An active participant in communication and personal relationship organizations, her research concerns friendship, competition in close relationships, and interpersonal communication.